Afraid To Let Go

For Parents of Adult Addicts and Alcoholics

Mary Crocker Cook, D.Min., LMFT, CADCII

Afraid to Let Go

© 2012 Mary Crocker Cook

ISBN: 978-1-61170-092-3

Email: marycook@connectionscounselingassociates.com

Printed in the USA and UK on acid-free paper.

To purchase additional copies of this book go to:
www.rp–author.com/mcook

Robertson Publishing™
www.RobertsonPublishing.com

Acknowledgements

Thank you to my co-editors, Howard Scott Warshaw and Robin Nakamura

This book is for parents who are Afraid to Let Go because they do not know how to set boundaries with their addicted adult children without feeling crippling anxiety, or walling themselves off to make separation possible

CONTENTS

Working definition of Codependency :
At its heart, Codependency is a set of behaviors developed to manage the anxiety that comes when our primary attachments are formed with people who are inconsistent or unavailable in their response to us. Our anxiety-based responses to life can include over-reactivity, image management, unrealistic beliefs about our limits, and attempts to control the reality of others to the point where we lose our boundaries, self-esteem, and even our own reality. Ultimately, Codependency is a chronic stress disease, which can devastate our immune system and lead to systemic and even life-threatening illness.

PART ONE

At its heart, Codependency is a set of behaviors developed to manage the anxiety that comes when our primary attachments are formed with people who are inconsistent or unavailable in their response to us.

PART TWO

Our anxiety-based responses to life can include over-reactivity, image management, unrealistic beliefs about our limits, and attempts to control the reality of others to the point where we lose our boundaries, self-esteem, and even our own reality.

PART THREE
Ultimately, Codependency is a chronic stress disease, which can devastate our immune system and lead to systemic and even life-threatening illness.

PART FOUR
Recovery is Possible

INTRODUCTION

A NOTE TO PARENTS

If you are Codependent you are not a "control freak"
or a "helicopter parent" or suffering from "empty nest" syndrome.
You are terrified.

You are not Codependent simply because your adult child is an addict or alcoholic.

All parents of addicted children of any age are terrified, confused, feel out of control, lose sleep and dread the phone calls at 3:00 in the morning.

My son is a 26 year old addicted to coke. So he says but I suspect more. He's been in rehab twice. His girlfriend is a TV journalist, doing very well but he just binged this weekend and they're done now.

His truck is broken down, his boss is a drug addict and he won't answer the phone. She's asked him to leave, he won't so she's staying in a hotel. Not sure where this is going. Expect her to call police to get him out. Seems people die in those situations. I don't understand "detaching" etc. I feel if there is any possible hope to offer him help to get better, I would because I don't think I could live with the alternative, i.e. suicide. I'd rather have a drug addict for a son than a dead son. Does that make any sense? http://www.dailystrenght.org

Families change in response to the presence of addiction and alcoholism, and in many ways in response to the kind of fears that this mother expresses. As the chaos increases, the family structure changes. There are many talented family theorists and addiction authors who describe the addicted family system well. They address the family roles, the shifts in power and control, and the communication styles to which we adapt to survive.

This is an overview of patterns that disrupt attachment in families, and I have included some resources for further reading in the back of the text.

There are marvelous articles, books and resources in the community that address families who are having trouble "launching" their adult children (whether or not they are addicts). These texts look at the sociological changes and economic challenges that have made this process difficult, and prolonged adolescence. These resources also provide excellent practical ideas on how to live with your adult child.

The purpose of this book is to assist the parent who is struggling with attachment issues, especially those who have had difficulty in their primary relationship with separation and bonding prior to even having their own children. For the purposes of this discussion we will define these individuals as "Codependent" parents, those who have exhibited these patterns prior to becoming parents.

*This book is for parents who are **Afraid to Let Go** because they do not know how to set boundaries with their addicted adult children without feeling crippling anxiety, or walling themselves off to make separation possible.*

My only child, my 26 year old son, is addicted to prescription pain meds-or at least they started out as prescription and the past year and a half have been heartbreaking. He had an accident and illness for which he was hospitalized and given morphine and sent home with opiates and it got worse and worse. The family, (his dad and I and his fiancés mother) all confronted him and he went crazy and denied it. He then a few months later came to us and asked for help. He refused in patient treatment but did go for a couple of weeks of Methadone -his choice of treatment. I don't think it made a difference as he was still smoking pot and who knows what else.

Meanwhile, he has stolen from me, from his fiancé, (and they have since broken up) written bad checks and avoided dealing with the legal repercussions, and is living with whoever will have him—my guess

is more addicts. This is a kid who is brilliant, was hard working, responsible and is now just dysfunctional, not working for almost a year, getting food stamps and it is breaking my heart. He doesn't even call to let me know he is alive, which may not seem odd for some sons but he always called at least once a week just to say hi. Now he won't let me see him. I am sure he is ashamed of the way he has treated those who love him.

I know I can't make him better but I sure am having trouble accepting that there is nothing I can do. I went to Alanon since we don't have a Narcanon group locally and I just had a lot of trouble with the idea of letting go. I keep thinking he has hit bottom but it keeps getting worse and I fear he will end up dead. I am terrified and heartbroken. Sorry to be such a whiner, I just would really love to hear from other parents of adult drug addicts to know how they dealt with the pain and fear. I have thought about turning him in since he has notices about the bad checks because I think he would be less danger to himself if he is in prison, but I fear that he will get even worse if he has access to what is there. I also know that he could get really crazy and be put in the state mental hospital for prisoners and they would just keep him sedated and exacerbate the problem. Does anyone have any experience that they can share with me? *http://www.dailystrenght.org*

If you are reading this book, it is likely that you have been concerned about your adult child for several years. It is also likely that you have already paid for several treatment episodes in residential or outpatient treatment. You have probably consulted with experts in the addictions field or attended family groups for family members of addicts/alcoholics, Al-Anon or Codependents Anonymous.

And you can't "let go." You can't "detach with love." You can't let them "hit bottom." You can't seem to implement the strategies you have learned when you are faced with your adult child's chaos and anxiety. When you try to do this, it makes you physically and emotionally ill. The anxiety and fear become unbearable.

Despite your fear of "becoming an enabler," you may continue to:

- call the bail bondmen one more time
- pay off the dealer
- hire another attorney
- take the grandkids again
- let them move in again
- pay their rent, their tickets, their credit cards
- hear yourself blaming the treatment professionals, the counselors, the system, the ex-spouse or partner while you may secretly be terrified that it's really your fault

Why can't you just "let go"?

If you are struggling with Codependency, your relationship with your child is not the only relationship where you experience a loss of self, a loss of control and tremendous over-reactivity. It's not the only place you display intrusive or impulsive behavior to "help" in situations, even when your assistance has not been requested.

If you are Codependent, this is not the first relationship in which you "over-give," resulting in feelings of resentment, and making sacrifices to give them what you decide they "need." After all if you don't, who will?

If you are Codependent you are not a "control freak" or a "helicopter parent" or suffering from "empty nest" syndrome. You are just simply terrified.

In this text I will be using the following definition of Codependency:

At its heart, Codependency is a set of behaviors developed to manage the anxiety that comes when our primary attachments are formed with people who are inconsistent or unavailable in their response to us. Our anxiety-based responses to life can include over-reactivity, image management, unrealistic beliefs about our

limits, and attempts to control the reality of others to the point where we lose our boundaries, self-esteem, and even our own reality. Ultimately, Codependency is a chronic stress disease, which can devastate our immune system and lead to systemic and even life-threatening illness.

Codependent parents developed their parenting styles in response to the attachments they formed with their own caregivers. We will talk about this in greater depth, but simply put; if you can't trust your attachments to those closest to you, how can you trust your attachment to your own adult child? We don't trust that our children truly love us, or would actually choose the relationship with us anymore than we trust the other adults around us. We are intuitively afraid that if we let go, they will not willingly return. That's why we allow them to depend on us or need us. That's why we resist allowing ourselves to depend on them.

Again, this did not start with our children. This lack of trust in relationship attachment came way before we were parents - having children just up the ante. These feelings are heightened and triggered more often when the people we are most afraid of losing are inconsistent themselves. Addicted adult children are erratic in their availability and response. They disappear for stretches of time with no response to any form of communication until they show up (without warning) in a "crisis." Their response level may depend on their level of intoxication, or perhaps incarceration has made them unavailable. Worst of all, the separation we fear most becomes permanent due to death from an overdose, or violence.

"My son is addicted to alcohol. He has cirrhosis of the liver. He continues to use, even after treatment. I have had a hard time letting go. He has overdosed 2 times, recently. I was there to get him help. He lived, but they spent over an hour to revive him. It is coming to a point, that all is left for me to do, is let go. He lives with me, but is gone now, still using. He called and ask me to give him a ride to pick up someone. I said no. I am going to bed and putting my phone off of the hook. I need rest and sleep or I will be no good for anything. Let go and let God, I will

do. I have worked so hard with my own efforts, to no avail. Yes, he is still alive and I am grateful. But, he is still using more and more, and I feel like I have lost him anyway. So heartbreaking." *www.dailystrenght.org*

If I grew up with parents who were inconsistent or unresponsive in their behavior toward me, and my adult child behaves the SAME WAY, it makes sense that the same anxiety I experienced as a child would surface when I am faced with the same situation. The same coping mechanisms I developed as a child with my own unavailable parent would surface again when my adult child becomes inconsistent and unreliable.

It sounds logical, doesn't it?

It feels insane.

This "re-enactment" of childhood attachment issues is the reason the treatment professionals, working with your addicted adult child, may treat YOU in the same way they treat your child. In fact, unless you address these underlying issues, your adult child may respond to treatment and become far more stable than you. Then there is a real danger of your accidentally sabotaging your adult child's recovery by trying to "earn" their relationship with you, or trying to keep them from being angry with you.

Lastly, Codependency for parents is a deadly serious issue that can literally kill you. The constant stimulation of your "fight or flight" responses triggered by your adult child can cause serious, long term, systemic illness due to damage to your immune system. It's not their addiction that kills you, it's your constant anxiety about the separation or loss that weakens you. Ultimately it can be fatal.

There is hope. I firmly believe that knowledge is power. When you understand what is happening to you, you have the choice to heal. When you invest the time to learn more about your underlying Codependency, you become perfectly capable of practicing the appropriate behavior and mental attitude to take care of yourself and make room for your adult child to meet you in a more mutually cooperative and equitable way.

After 25 years working with families, I believe in the power of family attachment. In most cases the relationships survive. The parent-child attachment is still intact, despite the erratic behaviors attached to their alcohol and drug use. *Their unavailability has nothing to do with their attachment to you or love for you.* It is my hope that this text will help you believe this.

This text is based on several assumptions:

- The majority of parents love their adult children and are "hard wired" to protect them.

- The majority of parents play out attachment issues with their adult children that are multi-generational. In other words, they parent in response, or even in reaction to, the way they were parented. There is no "blame" in this text. It is meant to be informative and to create a foundation for understanding and healing, not an indictment of parents.

- The majority of parents want their adult children to be healthy and stable, knowing that there will be a time when they will no longer be there to protect them.

I am going to introduce you to Attachment Theory, which is research based. I feel that this is an important key to understanding the foundation of attachment and Codependency.

Afraid to Let Go

PART ONE

At its heart, Codependency is a set of behaviors developed to manage the anxiety that comes when our primary attachments are formed with people who are inconsistent or unavailable in their response to us.

CHAPTER ONE

Foundations for Attachment Patterns

Let's begin by taking a look at what experts on child development have to say about forming healthy parent/child attachment bonds.

Why Does Attachment Matter?

Secure bonding and attachment between caregivers and their children sets the foundation for our future connections with others. Bonding generally refers to the parents' emotional investment in their child, which builds and grows with repeated meaningful shared experiences. Attachment usually refers to the tie between the infant and parents, which the child actively initiates and participates in. The quality of attachment largely determines the child's developing sense of self and approach to the world environment.

Psychologist John Bowlby, the first attachment theorist, describes attachment as a "lasting psychological connectedness between human beings."(1)

Beginning with John Bowlby (2), Attachment Theory offers the following themes:

1. A psychology based on the opposing tendencies of attachment and separation/loss. There is always a tension between our need to feel connected and have roots, and our need to develop which will push us out of our "safe" zone. I would argue that we need one (safety) to fully embrace the other (separation).

2. The individual's need for secure attachment in order to successfully reach out and explore one's inner world and outer environment. Knowing I have a safe harbor allows me to risk

entering deeper waters, trusting that when I come home to familiar waters I will recognize myself and the people who love me who are waiting for me to return.

3. The persistence of attachment needs throughout life. Bowlby points out that we never outgrow the need for secure attachments. Having a "home base" is key to personal and professional development, whereas lack of a home base can create almost intolerable anxiety.

4. The negative consequences of early disruption of bonding or attachment. Research shows early disruption of our ability to trust our attachments to others has life-long consequences. Up to 2/3 of people maintain consistent attachment style from childhood to adult relationships.

5. The caregiver's capacity to maintain loving presence and to accept protest is of vital importance to a child's mental health. *Accept protest* means letting the child express anger and frustration openly and without loss of parental love or intimacy.

Researchers point out that the ability to withstand separation has not had the same focus as establishing the original attachment. Yet, clinicians like Mary Ainsworth point out the parent's ability to accept protest without retaliation or excessive anxiety is a key determinant of secure attachment. (3) The child must be welcomed back with unconditional intimacy.

Parent's must resolve their own attachment needs in order to tolerate the child's growing need to differentiate (establish a "self" apart from the parent). Anxiously attached parents are threatened by the child's needs for "space" and may smother them, whereas avoidantly attached parents find the child's resistance or protests painful and then withdraw from the child.

What does it look like when a parent cannot connect this way due to her own interrupted attachment history?

Little Jeremy is quietly playing with his blocks, occasionally looking over to the kitchen to make sure his mom is still there. Mom is preoccupied while doing last night's dishes. She is tired of her husband's drinking and feels like saying something, but she dreads the fight that will unfold when she does. She looks over and sees Jeremy playing and has an urge to hug him, unaware that she is looking for comfort for herself. As she reaches out to pick Jeremy up he protests, wanting to continue playing with his toys.

Mom reacts as though she has been slapped by Jeremy. Feeling rejected, she roughly drops him back to the floor and heads back to the bedroom. Jeremy notices she is leaving and becomes anxious. He starts to cry for her. Angry with Jeremy, mom lets him cry for a while to "punish" him before returning to the den to pick him up.

We need to bond without being swallowed up. This contributes to our development of autonomy and creativity.

We need to separate without feeling abandoned. Caregivers remain attentive to the child's cues for reengagement.

Secure attachments develop as a result of consistent and accurate response between the caregiver and child. This requires the caregiver to be emotionally, cognitively, and physically present in a predictable and meaningful way in order to participate in the developing relationship over time.

Characteristics of Secure Attachment

- Safe Haven: When the child feels threatened or afraid, he or she can return to the caregiver for comfort and soothing.

- Secure Base: The caregiver provides a secure and dependable base for the child to explore the world.

- Proximity Maintenance: The child strives to stay near the caregiver, thus keeping the child safe.

- Separation Distress: When separated from the caregiver, the child will become upset and distressed.

Parental attunement and responsiveness has been documented on a physiological level as well. The heart rates of securely attached infants and their mothers in the Ainsworth's "Strange Situation" (See Appendix) parallel each other, whereas they do not with insecurely attached. Infants and their mothers (4). The mirroring of heart rates indicates the mother's sensitivity and involvement in her infant's perceived experience. Mothers of secure infants pick their babies up more quickly when they see signs of distress, play with them more, and generally seem more aware of them and their needs than parents of insecure infants. One such need is to be able to play "alone in the presence of the mother." To meet this need the mother must be capable of providing an unobtrusive background which enables self-exploration. (5) If the child is repeatedly interrupted by a demanding caregiver who seeks comfort and validation from the child, the child becomes prematurely and compulsively attuned to the demands of others. This child loses awareness of its own spontaneous needs and develops a false sense of self based on compliance and competence in meeting the needs of his/her caregivers.

John Bowlby: Attachment Theory Across Generations (Davidson Films, Inc.) http://www.youtube.com/watch?v=8ljZ4a8Uc8Q&feature=related

Michele is the youngest of five children. Her mother had been over stressed with no extended family support and the family lived in survival mode throughout Michele's childhood. Due to financial hardship and time limitations, Michele was not able to participate in after school activities and never had the chance to pursue her desire to take dancing lessons. Once Michele became a parent she swore that her children would never miss out on an opportunity. It creates enormous conflict between Michele and her daughter, Amber, when her daughter begs to stay home and play with her toy ponies instead of go to Gymboree class. Amber is realizing that her mommy becomes very sad and withdrawn for the rest of the night if Amber doesn't go to class, and then she feels sad herself. Amber misses her mom and begins to go to class without complaining so her mommy will be "happy" and then play with her the rest of the night.

Pediatrician and Psychoanalyst D.W. Winnicott pointed out that the need for privacy and occasional freedom from structure for "unstructured play" are necessary over the course of the life span. In childhood this is crucial to develop a *self*. (6) We never outgrow the need to regroup and think our own thoughts, just as we never outgrow the need for attachment and a secure base from which to explore the world.

Secure attachment is associated with an internalized sense of lovability, of being worthy of care, of being effective in eliciting care when required, and a sense of personal efficacy in dealing with most stressors independently. Secure preschoolers develop an understanding of other people's thoughts and emotions, leading to empathy (7).

The implications of this are powerful!

When I can TRUST the people close to me, I translate this to mean I am WORTH being loved and cared about. Because I have the "safety net" created by a trusted support system I feel like I can tackle stressors in my life and be effective. Because my caregivers have been accurately attuned to me emotionally and reflected my thoughts back to me accurately, I can TRUST myself to read the thoughts and feelings of others accurately because I recognize those thoughts and feelings. The ability to recognize and share in the feelings of others is empathy.

Attunement and Why It's Important
http://www.youtube.com/watch?v=URpuKgKt9kg&feature=related

When we don't have this secure foundation we become anxiously attached codependents who don't trust the attachment of and fear that they will abandon us, or we become avoidantly attached codependents who don't allow ourselves to attach to or depend on those who will "inevitably" leave us. Ultimately we are not attuned to ourselves or others and we translate that to mean we aren't worth being loved or attended to. This leads to life-long patterns of self-abandonment.

When Attachment Gets Interrupted

There are so many reasons that early attachment can get interrupted. Below are a few of the more common reasons:

- Extended periods of illness (parent or child)
- Hospitalization due to physical or mental illness
- Placement in the foster care system
- Serious mental illness creating emotional and mental unavailability
- Abusive relationships that absorb the majority of the caretaker's energy
- Incarceration
- Alcohol/Drug addiction
- Military service

None of these reasons have anything to do with LOVE for the child. Unfortunately the child cannot possibly know this. The child winds up believing that the unavailable parent is not available due to some defect within the child. We believe that if we were "enough" the parent would CHOOSE to be available.

This begins the "going to the hardware store to get milk" pattern we talk about in Al-Anon. In this analogy, we go to the hardware store to get milk, which is not sold at hardware stores.

When we realize milk is not available we:

- protest and demand more loudly that they get milk for us assuming they aren't listening or taking our needs seriously
- accuse them of having milk but withholding it from us
- believe that they would give us milk if we were somehow different or better

Sanity returns when we acknowledge that the store is not withholding milk but simply does not have it to sell. In reality, many of us spend years of our lives using every tool possible to "force" a response from our parents that they are not capable of giving. When we learn that they do not have it to give, we can stop futile demands that increasingly damage the relationship and our self-esteem over time. We can learn to accept what people CAN give rather than focus on what they are not capable of giving.

Amy has fought all her life for her mother's approval. She overhears her mother tell other people how proud she is of Amy, yet the direct feedback she receives consists of warnings to "not get too big for her britches," or not to "count her chickens before their hatched" whenever Amy announces a new professional undertaking. When Amy was honored as valedictorian in high school, her mother pointed out that there would be smarter kids at the college when Amy got there. She reminded Amy, "Don't think that just because you are a big fish in a little pond that there aren't bigger fish." Amy pushed herself so hard at work that she began to have conflicts with her coworkers, and her boss gently recommended that Amy see an Employee Assistance Counselor. By the second visit, the Counselor was clear that Amy would need longer term support and recommended a therapist that specialized in codependency issues.

Through the course of therapy, Amy began to explore her mother's history as a child which had been filled with lost dreams and broken promises. Her mother had closed off her heart to "possibility" a long time ago, and it became clear to Amy that her mother saw herself as protective of Amy by offering her such discouraging feedback. Over time, she learned that her mother was not capable of celebrating success with Amy, terrified that something would happen and Amy would get her heart broken the way she had earlier in life. Amy would need to seek out people who were not so afraid to share her latest business ideas. It was not that her mother didn't love her or wasn't proud, she was simply too wounded and too scared to risk feeling Amy's joy.

Characteristics of Anxious or Ambivalent Attachment
(Anxious Codependent)

Research suggests that anxious attachment is a result of poor maternal availability or inconsistent responsiveness to the child. These children cannot depend on their mother (or caregiver) to respond in a consistent or timely manner when the child is in need or experiencing distress.

These parents tend to be poorly attuned to their children's needs, often ignoring them when they are distressed and intruding on them when they are playing contentedly. These parents offer interrupted or inconsistent parental care. When the parent feels calm, she responds to her child in a sensitive way; when she is angry, she expresses it openly with yelling and perhaps hitting. The parent's responses are internally consistent for them, but unfortunately unpredictable to anyone else, especially the child. *The child feels powerless to control or predict his/her experience* because the response will be unpredictably either supportive or hostile which may create learned helplessness and limit risk taking and exploration.

> Optimal Attachment with Daniel Siegel:
> http://www.youtube.com/watch?v=_XjXv6zseA0&feature=related

This is an impossible situation to maneuver because the rules for conduct and parental expectations are always shifting based on the caregiver's emotional regulation skills. I can go to hug my mom after school today and she will be either neutral or positive. However, when I do the same thing tomorrow I might be met with a hostile response: "Why are you bothering me? Leave me alone!"

Martin has always wanted children, promising himself that he would provide a different childhood than he had experienced with his alcoholic father. When his own son, Jorge, was born it was the happiest day of Martin's life. Martin never drinks to make sure his new son has it "better than I had." Unfortunately, without alcohol (Martin's only stress-management tool) Martin is increasingly moody and unpredictable at home. His wife, Lucia, spends a lot of energy trying to anticipate Martin's mood, including calling him before he leaves work to "get the lay of the land." Jorge, who is now 3 years old, adores his father and lights up the room every time he sees him. Some of the time, Martin is equally thrilled to see his son, no matter what kind of day he has had.

However, sometimes when Jorge runs up to the door, Martin is sharp with him – roughly dismisses him by telling him to "go away and play," or yells for Lucia to "come get the boy" in obvious annoyance at the child's demands. Jorge is crushed when this happens, and is confused. While Lucia tries to comfort him, Jorge still feels like he did something wrong by bothering his daddy.

Even when the child can force closeness and attention from the care-giver, once obtained it is often not soothing and may be punishing. Consequently the child remains persistently anxious or angry.

Because of the intermittent reinforcement for turning to the attach-ment figure for security (sometimes they respond and sometimes they don't), the need to be vigilant for her presence and loss is strong-ly reinforced. *The child's confidence in itself to respond appropriately to threats and self-soothe does not develop adequately* as all of its coping mechanisms are being developed to manage external threats to se-curity. This sets the foundation for later external choices to manage our anxiety, such as alcohol, drugs, or pornography. Certainly we are learning that trusting the people close to us will not be a realistic option, and more than likely we will pick relationships in the future that will reinforce that trust is not possible by picking unavailable, unpredictable partners.

Case Example:
An extreme example of this rage and impulsiveness was demon-strated by Clara Harris, who became overwhelmed by the threat of abandonment by her husband, David.

Clara Harris is an accomplished dentist and business woman, who was seen by others to be extremely competent, family-oriented, and even controlling. In 2002, Clara Harris discovered her husband, co-owner of their six successful dental practices, was carrying on an affair with the receptionist, Gail Bridges, a divorcee with three children of her own. As soon as Clara Harris found out about her husband's affair she did everything she could think of to save her marriage, which included willingness to lose herself and merge into her projection of her husband's fantasy partner. She:

- obtained detailed information from her husband on what attracted him to the other woman
- had a heart-to-heart talk with her husband about their marital problems.
- went to a salon and had her hair cut and lightened to blonde
- had her nails done
- joined a gym / health club
- hired a personal trainer.
- made a $5000 deposit for breast augmentation surgery and liposuction
- cooked her husband's favorite meals
- began having sex with him at least 3 times each night
- went shopping for sexy clothes
- bought seductive lingerie from Victoria's Secret
- took a leave of absence from her job at the couple's chain of dental clinics so she could devote all her time to her husband
- fired her husband's mistress, who worked as a receptionist at the same dental clinic as her husband
- persuaded her husband to agree to end his affair with the other woman
- had her stepdaughter buy her 2 relationship books
- hired a private investigator
- discussed seeing a marriage counselor

A truly anxious/ambivalent Codependent, Clara did all this in the space of 7 days, wasting no time. She found out about the affair on July 16th, and her husband confessed to the affair on July 17th. Clara's efforts to save her marriage might have succeeded, but by July 24th, David Harris was dead. Intent on doing everything she could to save her from the day she discovered his infidelity until the day David Harris was killed, Clara was unable to tolerate evidence that the affair had continued and the attachment remained threatened.

Clara Harris confronted her husband with his lover at a hotel. She then went outside, got in her Mercedes and proceeded to run over her husband again and again, circling the car over different parts of his body, crushing his legs, ribs and head. An eye witness to the crime stated that when Clara finished, she got out of her car and, in a final burst of anger, leaned over her husband's mangled, crushed body as he exhaled his last breath. "See what you made me do!" she screamed.

When interviewed later, it was clear that Clara had loved her husband "more than life" and just wanted to stop the pain she was feeling. Obliterating him was an attempt to obliterate her pain.

> Ambivalent Attachment with Daniel Siegel:
> http://www.youtube.com/watch?v=nGhZtUrpCuc&feature=related

Characteristics of Avoidant or Dismissive Attachment
(Avoidant Codependent)

Research indicates that when caregivers are consistently un-responsive, or even punishing when children seek closeness these children will show no preference between a caregiver and a complete stranger. *Children who are punished for relying on a caregiver will learn to avoid seeking help in the future.*

These parents are more brusque and functional in their handling, unresponsive to their child's needs or intolerant of a child's distress. Grossmann and Grossmann (8) studied parental interaction with babies identified as avoidant at 12 and 18 months. *Parents of avoidant babies interfered when their babies were already engrossed in play, and withdrew when their babies expressed negative feelings, especially toward the caregiver.* The children showed many expressions of uncertainty toward continued play. By contrast, parents of securely attached infants engaged in mutual play when the baby appeared to be at a loss for what to do next but watched quietly (with interest) when the infants did not need them. The avoidant child learns that seeking closeness through crying and clinging is futile. It actually results in parental withdrawal. Independence is reinforced and valued instead. As a result, attachment behaviors are relatively diminished and detachment behaviors become prominent.

Cherise was stunned when her husband announced his intention to file for divorce and move in with her best friend. Cherise was almost immobilized with grief now that she had lost BOTH people in her life she trusted. Managing two children, 5 and 7 years old, was overwhelming. Sammy, her 7 year old, looked very much like his father and had many of his mannerisms. There were times when his tone of voice or facial expression was a carbon copy of his father. Sammy was tearful and uncooperative with Cherise when she could muster up the energy to interact with him, which discouraged her from even trying. It was clear to both children that when they needed something it made mommy angry and she was "mean," especially to Sammy. Sammy learned to make breakfast for he and his sister instead of asking for help. He learned to help his sister get dressed before school, and encouraged her to "play quietly" when they were home so mommy could rest.

Maintaining physical closeness to the caregiver is necessary for any child's protection and nurturing, and a child's natural tendency is to withdraw from a perceived threat and approach the caretaker for safety and comforting. However, the avoidant child's caretaker (i.e., mother) *is* the threat, and punishes the approaching child with rejection. Thus, the child has learned to avoid any communication of dependence, presenting an irresolvable conflict between their instincts for safety and comfort and the pain of rejection. This lays the foundation for the increased detachment from their internal world which is so present in avoidant adults.

Avoidant Attachment with Daniel Siegel:
http://www.youtube.com/watch?v=qgYJ82kQIyg&feature=related

The Avoidant Codependent conflict is this: I *want* to allow myself to depend on someone who SAYS they love me, but my *experience* is whenever I become vulnerable or "needy" I get abandoned and hurt. So, I allow myself to attach to others to a point but always have a "Plan B" prepared for the inevitable disappointment of rejection. Of course the very act of having a "Plan B" means that I never fully ante up – I am never all the way "in" which leads to the separation. I'm convinced is inevitable anyway. I may be manifesting the very thing I fear most.

Marlene has been in a long distance relationship with Raj for the last two years and for most of that time has driven three hours to see him every weekend. To make this more comfortable, she has stored clothing and some personal effects at his home to make travel easier. Raj is very much in love with Marlene and has expressed often that he would like to have her move in with him and "take this relationship to the next level," including marriage. This creates tremendous anxiety for Marlene as she pictures herself being "swallowed up" by Raj, completely dependent on him in a new environment. As she agrees to this plan, she arranges to store all of her furniture rather than sell it on Craig's list, "just in case" everything goes south and she has to start all over again. In the process of making arrangements to move, Raj and Marlene start fighting every weekend. This triggers Marlene to finally say, "Forget it. I KNEW if I let myself depend on you, you would become a control freak," and break up with him.

In reality the act of detaching emotionally from relationships as protection is an empty gesture. Research (9) with surviving family members of victims of suicide or accidental death indicate that the most grief-stricken survivors were more detached from family than those who were least grief stricken. The detached survivors actually had more unresolved in their relationships, which created greater grief when the opportunity for resolution was suddenly and permanently denied. Remorse compounds the loss.

Avoidant Codependents are not obvious in that they may have a variety of social connections. They may have been children who used compensating strategies of compulsive caregiving, in which the child reassures the withdrawn and depressed parent that everything is all right, or compulsive compliance, in which the child becomes highly vigilant to the hostile and unpredictable parent's desires and complies promptly with them. These children may become "parentified" as a caretaker for their parent and may be able to anticipate and comply with the parent's needs before they are even formulated. (10, 11) Ultimately they become adolescents and adults who are emotionally insulated, intimacy-phobic and "compulsively self-reliant." (12) A consequence of this insulation is isolation. The underlying incentive for the avoiding aspect of detachment is fear of intimacy.

Carolyn has been staying home from school when her mother has a migraine since she was in elementary school. Her mother's migraines began shortly after her divorce and Carolyn's mother would become immobilized by her migraine, unable to take care of household responsibilities. Carolyn learned to anticipate the "signs" of an impending headache usually triggered by stress. She became very adept at managing her own meals and homework, asking for very little input from her mother. In fact, when her mother would come home from work, Carolyn would usually have dinner prepared and would spend whatever time was necessary listening as mom processed her day. Carolyn discovered she missed far less time at school when she adhered to this routine, so would turn down invitations to other people's homes if it would make her unavailable for her mother. Carolyn's mother consistently told others how close she felt to Carolyn as they "shared everything" with each other. In reality, Carolyn's mother knew very little about her daughter as they both ignored Carolyn's internal world.

CHAPTER TWO

CODEPENDENCY AND ATTACHMENT THEORY

I am certainly not the first to make the connection between codependency and attachment theory. Zimberoff and Hartman (13) indicate in their research that:

"the child who is repeatedly interrupted by a demanding caregiver, i.e., through the parental impingement phenomenon, becomes compulsively attuned to the demands of others, losing awareness of its own spontaneous needs and developing a false sense of self based on compliance and performance. This infant experiences his/her parents (and thus the world) as dangerous and frightening. This can be the genesis of codependency in adulthood… Seriously insecure attachment creates a dissociated core of the self, an absence of self. It reflects a breach in the boundaries of the self…"

Author Dr. Tian Dayton (14) provides her own definition of codependency using an integration of attachment theory (and Bowen family systems theory):

"Codependency, I feel, is fear-based and is a predictable set of qualities and behaviors that grow out of feeling anxious and therefore hypervigilant in our intimate relationships. It is also reflective of an incomplete process of individuation….Though codependency seems to be about caretaking or being overly attuned to the other person, it is really about trying to fend off our own anxiety."

Dr. Dayton believes that codependency and counterdependency (what I am labeling avoidant/dismissive attachment) are the result of attachment injuries, or relationship traumas as she calls it.

In his seminal book, *The Road Less Traveled*, M. Scott Peck explores the roles of fear of abandonment. Self-care — or the ability to recognize that you will get what you want only if you do some of the job yourself – is learned in the face of the child's elemental desire to be cared for totally. Our fundamental desire to merge struggles with the need to develop competence. Competence is scary, because it may indicate to our caretakers that we are ready to be "on our own" and we may find ourselves prematurely self-sufficient. Developing initiative and skills does not have to result in abandonment. With a secure home base we can venture out and return, trusting there will be a consistent welcome.

Most parents, even when they are otherwise relatively ignorant or callous, are instinctively sensitive to their children's fear of abandonment and will therefore, day in and day out, hundreds and thousands of times, offer their children needed reassurance: "You know Mommy and Daddy aren't going to leave you behind"; "Of course Mommy and Daddy will come back to get you"; "Mommy and Daddy aren't going to forget about you!" If these words are matched by deeds, month in and month out, year in and year out, by the time of adolescence, the child will have lost the fear of abandonment and in its stead will have a deep inner feeling that the world is a safe place in which to be, and protection will be there when it is needed. With this internal sense of the consistent safety of the world, such a child is free to delay gratification of one kind or another, secure in the knowledge that the opportunity for gratification, like home and parents, is always there, available when needed....(15)

Internal Working Models

The construct to explain how the early attachment experiences become long-term, lifelong traits is that of internal working models. With repetition over time, the infant is conditioned into generalizing his/her experiences into expectations for future relationship experience. Internal working models serve to regulate, interpret, and predict the parent/child attachment-related behavior, thoughts, and feelings in situations of loss, threat, isolation and dependency. A child constructs a working model of itself as valued and competent when parents as emotionally available and supportive of exploratory activities.

Samuel loves children and was thrilled to have both a son and a daughter. As his daughter, Sarah, becomes 9 years old she begins to struggle in math. Samuel has always loved math and at first he is confused by her apparent inability to master what, to him, are simple concepts. However, Samuel knows Sarah is bright and commits to patiently working with her every evening. In the process Samuel is communicating to Sarah that she is capable, that she CAN do the math, and he is committed to supporting her efforts even if it means hiring a tutor. Sarah is very clear that her struggle in math is completely separate from her value as a person and her father's attention and support are not conditional. Sarah's working model will be "I ask for support and I am responded to without shame." This will bode very well for her when she begins to look for a boyfriend because boys who speak to her with respect will be natural choices for her.

> Optimal Attachment with Daniel Siegel:
> http://www.youtube.com/watch?v=_XjXv6zseA0&feature=related

Conversely, a working model of self as devalued and incompetent develops from parents who are rejecting or ignoring thus interfering with exploration. The models of self and parents develop together, as complements of each other, and represent both sides of the relationship. (16)

Healthy development requires a child to update internal working models over time. In fact, "Bowlby repeatedly warned of the pathogenic illness causing] potential of working models that are not updated" (17). The expectations of one's parents and oneself at age one certainly adjusts and expands by age three, or ten, or eighteen. A parent may "reform," becoming more able to respond to his/her child's needs when life circumstances improve, leading the child to construct revised working models of self as valued and of parents as caring.

Manuel has spent the first 6 years of his son's life in and out of addiction rehabilitation centers. Manuel loves his son, Juan, very much but has broken many promises and has not been reliable. He knows Juan loves him also, but Juan is a little afraid of him and worries about whether or not Manuel will do what he promises to do. Manuel is committed to sobriety at this point in his life and has maintained 2 years clean and sober. The longer he remains sober the more he notices that Juan doesn't call him so many times to "remind" him before he visits. He notices that the transition between visits is smoother as Juan no longer clings to him, afraid he won't see Manuel again. The stronger the relationship with Juan becomes the more deeply committed Manuel is to his sobriety, realizing that he can have the relationship with Juan that he never had with his own father.

However, there is built-in resistance to changing models once they have become habitual and automatic. Expectations become self-fulfilling through biased expectations of upcoming experiences with parents, and through the process of relationship consistency (18). A parent's occasional failure to attend is not likely to undermine a child's confidence in their emotional availability, nor is her parent's occasional healthy caregiving likely to overcome a child's learned insecurity.

Eventually, the internal working models that drive our ways of acting and thinking become unconscious (inaccessible to consciousness) and thus inflexible and reactive.

The family experience of those who grow up anxious and fearful is characterized not only by uncertainty about parental support, but also by subtle yet strongly distorting parental pressures. For example, pressure on the child to act as caregiver for a parent; or to adopt, and thereby to confirm, a parent's working models of self, of child and of their relationship.

Jackie has known from a very young age that her parents worry a great deal about how they are seen as demonstrated by the familiar mantra, "What will people think?" Jackie is acutely aware of her mother's dependency on her pills, what she calls her "nerve medicine," and her mother frequently forgets obligations or even full sentences in the evening. Jackie is especially afraid to drive in the evening with her mother because her mother tends to drift into other lanes as she chats away oblivious to the havoc she is creating around her. Rather than address the pill abuse that creates this dangerous situation, Jackie points out that her mother's eyesight seems to be less sharp at night. She repeats this so often it becomes a family belief, and her father begins to do the driving in the evening. Jackie is well aware that an open discussion of a family "problem" would be met with denial and most likely she would be identified as having a bad attitude.

The family experience of those who grow up to become relatively secure and self-reliant is characterized not only by unfailing parental support but also by a steady yet timely encouragement toward increasing autonomy. There is a frank communication by parents of their models, their expectations for relationship rules and structure for themselves, for the child and for others. These working models are not only acknowledged but are open to be questioned and revised.

Brett and his sister Joyce have always enjoyed visits to their grandparent's house in the summer. They are able to fish and swim in the lake. Their grandparents are obviously thrilled to spend the time with them. Brett and Joyce have become increasingly worried about their single dad, Mike. He seems quiet, preoccupied, and can't remember his commitments. Last week he forgot to pick up Brett after baseball and another parent took him home. They share their concerns with their grandparents, Mike's parents, and the grandparents become concerned. They are hearing signs of depression that they knew Mike had struggled with when the children were younger. When their dad comes for a visit, the family sits down to have dinner and the grandparent's help the children to tell their dad what they are noticing and tell him they are worried. Mike is able to hear their concerns without becoming angry and, after his initial denial, agrees to see a doctor.

Sometimes when our experience does not match the acceptable "reality" our parents pressure us to adopt, one defense is to change the model by changing the identity of the person (e.g., an attachment figure) involved. For example, a child may divert hostile feelings toward the parent which are inconsistent with the parent's working model of relationships, toward another less formidable person like a neighbor or a coach. *Obviously Daddy can't be unavailable – the coach is stupid for scheduling the game at that time.*

Some children produce defensive self-blame by taking anger they initially felt toward the attachment figure and redirect it towards themselves. *Daddy would be available if I was smarter.*

They may compulsively attempt to offer caregiving to others (including the parent), diverting attention from their own unmet attachment needs. *If I make Daddy laugh or bring him his beer he might want to come to my games.*

The child's response to negative parental treatment can be generalized as follows: The avoidant/dismissive child develops a deactivating strategy to ward off stressful experiences. The anxious/ambivalent child develops a hypervigilance strategy to detect and disarm them.

These patterns, while deeply embedded in the unconscious, remain active in driving behavioral choices. This is the general foundation for adult codependency.

Internal working models can be changed over time, as documented by changes in attachment classification. However, changing working models requires the individual to reassess some deeply embedded beliefs. The more deeply embedded the working model, the more profound any change becomes. Changing a working model based on early traumatic events requires revisions and reinterpretations of many related assumptions and beliefs.

That in turn requires enough security to risk the freedom to explore one's fundamental foundations. Thus, changing one's working model requires us to uncover our early experiences and create "corrective experiences" to replace the originally embedded fearful ones. (19) For example, hypervigilance based on parental inconsistency in childhood (e.g., "I expect my mother to explode in rage unpredictably any moment"), would need to be corrected by current experiences of secure attachments in the present that are predictable. My defense mechanism, hypervigilance, would no longer be necessary if my relationship choices became healthier.

Debbie has been seeing a therapist to treat her Post Traumatic Stress symptoms developed in response to a 10-year relationship. During those 10 years her children had experienced her as irritable, having mood swings, over reacting when startled and yelling, having physical pain which made her too tired to play with them and occasional periods where she would not get off the couch. However, as Debbie participates in her support groups, sees a therapist and is stabilized on medication she is becoming far more predictable. When the children have to give her "bad news" like a poor school grade, she is able to get into solution with the child and work to improve the grade. When she is having a difficult day, she is able to tell the children what is happening rather than acting it out in rejecting ways so they will leave her alone. Over time, the children notice that they are more comfortable having friends over to the house, and don't worry about her when they are gone. In fact, they are starting to take her for granted the way most children take their parent's for granted. In Debbie's case, it is a good sign when they forget to call on time because they are paying attention to their own lives instead of monitoring her!

CHAPTER THREE

FAMILY DYNAMICS THAT CREATE DISRUPTED ATTACHMENTS

Family systems theory is a theory of human behavior that views the family as an emotional unit. It is the nature of a family that its members are intensely connected emotionally. Often people feel distant or disconnected from their families, but this is more feeling than fact.

Family members so profoundly affect each other's thoughts, feelings and actions that it often seems as if people are living under the same "emotional skin." People try to get each other's attention, approval and support as they react to each other's needs, expectations and distress. This connectedness and reactivity make the functioning of family members interdependent. This means a change in one person's functioning is followed by changes in the functioning of others. (Think of a mobile – if you touch one part of it, the whole thing moves.) Families differ somewhat in the degree of interdependence but it is always present, even when family members are physically separated by great distances.

Emotional interdependence most likely evolved to promote the cohesiveness and cooperation families require to protect, shelter, and feed their members. Heightened tension can intensify the positive parts of cooperation and this can lead to greater cohesion. However, when family members get anxious the anxiety can escalate by spreading infectiously like a virus among them. As anxiety goes up, the emotional connectedness of family members becomes more stressful than comforting. Eventually one or more members feel overwhelmed isolated or out of control. The tragedy of anxiety is that it turns the very attachments protecting us from stress into a major *source* of stress.

Clinical problems or symptoms usually develop during periods of heightened and prolonged family tension. The level of tension depends on the stress a family encounters, how a family adapts to the stress and on a family's connection with extended family and social networks. *Tension increases the activity of one or more relationship patterns.* Symptoms develop according to which patterns are most active. The higher the tension, the greater the chance symptoms will be severe and several people will be vulnerable to problems such as depression, alcoholism, affairs, or physical illness.

Family Patterns

High Intensity vs. Shutdown/Dissociation

When family members become emotionally overwhelmed and have no way of staying safe, they may shut down or dissociate (freeze/flight). This is an unconscious attempt to protect themselves in much the same way as a circuit breaker flips when high wattage overwhelms a circuit and threatens to cause damage. This alternating pattern of high intensity and numbing becomes a quality that underlies many personal and family dynamics. It is the black and white pattern spoken of so often in addiction circles, the Jekyll/Hyde syndrome that characterizes the alternating worlds of the dysfunctional family system. Swings between high intensity and shutting down or dissociating characterize the trauma response and become central to the operational style of the family. "All or nothing" tends to characterize the family that contains trauma.

Janelle found Allen charming, funny, smart, ambitious, and incredibly handsome when they met at work. He was a sales rep assigned to her company, and she increasingly looked forward to his visits hoping he would stop in around lunch time and ask her out. Sure enough, everything unfolded in the storybook way Janelle had hoped for, and within six months Janelle was on her honeymoon. Janelle and Allen were in their late thirties so decided to start a family right away. Nature cooperated and within a year they had twin girls. During the pregnancy Janelle had noticed a pattern in Allen's behavior. He would be

up and positive for about six weeks, and then became sullen, unmotivated and argumentative for several weeks. As the stress increased and the financial demands of a family became more intense, the cycles became more intense. By the time the girls were in preschool, Janelle had trained them how to play and whether or not to even talk based on Allen's mood. Janelle was terrified that Allen was going to hurt the children in a rage, since he had pushed and hit her on occasion. When Allen was tense the entire family shut down.

Over Functioning vs. Under Functioning

In a maladaptive attempt to maintain family balance, some family members over function in order to compensate for the under functioning of others. Over functioning can wear many hats; parentified children may try to take care of younger siblings when parents drop the ball or strive to restore order or dignity when the family is rapidly slipping. Spouses may over function to maintain order and "keep the show on the road" while the unavailable partner falls in and out of normal functioning. Others in the system may freeze like a deer in headlights, unable to get their lives together and make useful choices. The learned helplessness associated with the trauma response, in which one comes to feel that nothing they can do will make a difference, can become an operational style that manifests as under functioning. It is possible the unstable person (along with others in the system) may even over-function at times to make up for periods of under-functioning.

Helen increasingly struggled with her anxiety. When she was younger she would get paralyzed by anxiety, but only in certain situations. As time went on she found herself experiencing panic attacks in historically non-threatening places, like the time she abandoned her shopping cart in Safeway and ran to the car. As a result, Helen was less and less able to attend her children's school functions, terrified she would panic and embarrass herself and the children. This was hard on them, and increasingly Helen's husband Carlos felt responsible to make sure he took time off work to be available for these events. He could feel the resentment inside as he had to return to work after dinner to take care of his unfinished projects. He struggled with feeling "alone" in the marriage, Helen seemed like another child for him to take care of! Helen felt Carlos' disappointment and distance from her, which only increased her anxiety and dread that she would be left alone at some point.

Enmeshment/Disengagement

Enmeshment or fusion (Anxious/ambivalent attachment style) is generally seen as an attempt to ward off feelings of abandonment. It is a relational style that lacks boundaries and discourages differences or disagreement, seeing them not as healthy and natural but disloyal and threatening. Dissension is not well tolerated and disagreement discouraged. The unspoken rule is "don't rock the boat."

Tony immigrated to the US, and has worked all of his life in anticipation of bringing his sons into the family moving business with him. Tony was thrilled by the company's success and proudly told people how one day the company would be run as "a family." Tony became increasingly worried because his oldest son, Pasquale, would become quiet when Tony would talk about the business, and resisted offers to come and "hang out" with his dad at the office. Tony's wife, Sophie, was also worried because she knew Tony had his heart set on Pasquale as the future business owner. Sophie was aware that Pasquale was a talented musician, and she had been approached by Pasquale's voice teacher to consider helping Pasquale apply for music scholarships to good colleges. Sophie had not told Tony about this, afraid of his disappointment. Instead Sophie would tell Pasquale how much she enjoyed his "hobby" because it made him happy, and pointed out that his music would be a good "hobby" to pursue to balance his work and home life as he got older. It was very clear to Pasquale if he went to college at all it would be to study business management and he was expected to use this training to advance the family. After everything his father had sacrificed for the family, upsetting and disappointing him was simply not an option.

Disengagement (Avoidant/dismissive attachment style) is the other side of enmeshment or fusion. Family members see avoiding subjects, people, places and things as the way to avoid pain and keep their inner worlds from erupting. This leads to emotional disengagement. Family members move into their own emotional and psychological orbits and they don't share their inner worlds with each other. This may give rise to covert alliances where a couple of family members ally and form covert bonds. This pattern can lead to the sense that we are roommates leading parallel lives instead of an interdependent.

Daniel and his three brothers have always been rowdy. They were fortunate to have such hardy parents to absorb their various escapades. However, their father Lou, had quite a temper when pushed too far or when he felt his authority was challenged, so the boys were careful to observe that line and not cross it. Their mother, Cindy, was efficient by nature and not particularly nurturing. Cindy would express love by making sure they had clean clothes and food in the house, even if she didn't always feel like preparing it herself. One afternoon the boys came home from school and found their mother crying in the kitchen. They were astonished and frightened. Daniel, as the oldest, instinctively took the lead and tried to engage Cindy. Through her tears she blurted out that their father had been arrested that afternoon for embezzlement and she didn't have enough money for bail so he would not be coming home. The boys were stunned and confused, unsure how to help her. They assured her there must be some mistake and he would be home soon.

The next morning Lou was on the front page with a list of damning evidence that made it pretty clear that he had been caught red-handed. Cindy simply folded the paper in half and left it on the table for the boys to read, never mentioning the article or the evidence again. Cindy quietly attended the trial and ultimately accepted that Lou would be away for the next ten years and she was now a single parent. Cindy never discussed this with the boys, she simply mentioned their father would not be home for a very long time and that 16 year-old Daniel would need to get a part time job after school to help support the family. It was clear to the boys that their job was to mind their own business, do their school work and not cause her any trouble.

Impulsivity vs. Rigidity

When emotional and psychological pain cannot get talked out, it often gets acted out through impulsive behaviors.

Impulsive behavior can lead to chaos when a pain filled inner world surfaces in action. Painful feelings that are too hard to sit with explode into the container of the family and get acted out. Blame, anger, rage, emotional, physical or sexual abuse, collapsing into helplessness, withdrawal or yelling, over or under spending and sexual anorexia or promiscuity are all variations of acting out emotional and psychological pain in dysfunctional ways that create chaos.

Rigidity is an attempt to manage that chaos both inwardly and outwardly. Adults in an addictive/traumatizing family system may tighten up on rules and routines in an attempt to counteract or ward off the feeling of falling apart inwardly or outwardly. And family members may tighten up in their personal styles becoming both controlled and controlling. There is no middle ground where strong feelings can be talked over or even explode momentarily but then be talked through toward some sort of tolerable resolution. Impulsive behavior is a manifestation of high intensity and rigidity is a manifestation of shutting down, clamping down or being physically present but psychically absent, following empty forms and rules. Again, the tendency is to alternate between black and white thinking, feeling and behaving with no shades of gray, reflecting the family's problems with regulation.

Nate had always struggled with his temper, especially when he was drunk. He had been arrested a number of times for drunk and disorderly behavior in public and assault as a result of bar fights. Nate could be violent with his sons as well. While he prided himself on never hitting a woman, he could be brutal with his sons when riled. He was ashamed the next morning when he noticed their black eyes and would vow to himself to not let it happen again. Of course, it always did. This was especially true when he would be angry at his boss and felt powerless to confront him about the unfairness in the workplace. Instead he would drink to "de-stress" and then wind up fighting with his sons.

Nate had a cousin who joined Alcoholic Anonymous and since then his life seemed to have less stress and he seemed to be happier. Desperate to change his life, Nate also joined Alcoholic Anonymous and stopped drinking. However, unlike his cousin, he couldn't seem to shake the stress. So instead of drinking he decided to begin to impose more control over the family in the evening to make sure he would have less aggravation. He was afraid if he let them aggravate him he would drink again. So he began to impose earlier bed times, banish them to their rooms to do their homework and bark at them if they were making too much noise when he was watching T.V. They always had to watch his shows now, because he needed to "let go" of his stress. While the boys were relieved they weren't getting beaten anymore, the atmosphere in the house was only slightly better. In some ways, Nate was worse to live with than before.

Grandiosity vs. Low Self Worth

Feelings of low self worth and shame can plague those within the addicted or overwhelmed family system. Not feeling normal, experiencing themselves as different from other families and hiding the painful truth of family dysfunction can all contribute to family members feeling bad about themselves.

Grandiosity is a common defense against feelings of worthlessness. Feelings of helplessness, frustration, shame and inadequacy get covered up with grandiose schemes and fantasies about what they are "going to do." Family members may not understand how to take baby steps toward success or getting their lives together. Frustrated and disheartened they may take refuge in grandiose ideas of themselves and their plans in life as a way of warding off ever-growing fears that their lives are somewhat unmanageable or they cannot seem to get things to work out for them.

Jerry had always been known as the family dreamer or "Mr. Big Idea." His wife, Patty, had tried to support whatever get-rich-quick scheme Jerry came up with, afraid to disappoint him or face accusations of being selfish and "holding him back." As a result, the family endured regular financial highs and lows. When times were good they moved to a better neighborhood. When Jerry would lose money they would move to poorer one. They moved down far more often than up. This was hard on the children because they were always starting over, having to make new friends and never feeling completely stable. However, they knew the family rule: don't challenge daddy's new plan. Whatever the plan, they were expected to be enthusiastic and listen to their father talk for hours about "when our ship comes in" and his latest plan to "make it big."

Denial vs. Despair

Addicted or traumatized families are often threatened by what they perceive to be the looming destruction of their family as they know it. Their very place in the world is being threatened; the ground beneath them is beginning to move. Denial is a dysfunctional attempt to put a good face on a bad situation. They deny the impact addiction is having on the family system. They deny the presence of the "pink elephant" who is taking up ever increasing amounts of space. Reality gets rewritten as family members attempt to make it less threatening; to cover up their ever growing despair. Family members often collude in this denial and anyone who attempts to spotlight the harsh reality of addiction may be perceived as disloyal. They run in place to keep up appearances (to themselves as well as others) while feeling a sense of despair constantly nipping at their heels. Again we witness the cycles between extremes that so characterize chaotic family systems.

Janet and Al share a tumultuous relationship fueled by alcohol. Al's drinking has become increasingly disruptive to the family. Janet and their three children walk on emotional "egg shells." One evening (after drinking heavily) Al explodes in rage over unwashed dishes. Janet grabs the children and runs to a back bedroom to hide as Al terrorizes them by pounding on the door and screaming threats. Janet locates a cell phone but instead of calling 911 she calls for pizza delivery telling the children that since Daddy is mad they will have a picnic in the bedroom. She engages them in the "picnic" by sending the oldest child out to get the pizza when it is delivered since Al had gone out to the garage to refuel. It never occurred to Janet to leave the house. In fact, she was willing to send the oldest child out to the door rather than face her husband herself. By engaging the children in the "picnic," she teaches them the same denial skills her mother had given her when her own father was abusive.

Caretaking vs. Neglect

Caretaking can be an attempt to attend to, in another person, what needs to be attended to within the self. We unconsciously transfer (displace) our own anxiety or pain onto someone else. Then we set about attending to "their" symptoms rather than to our own. It is a form of care that is motivated by our own unidentified needs (such as anxious or avoidant attachment needs) rather than a genuine awareness of the needs of others. Because this is the case, neglect can be its dark side. We neglect or don't see a real need in another person because we can't identify a real need within the self.

Rachel had always had a soft heart. Even as a child she would bring home wounded birds or injured cats, hoping she would be allowed to keep them and nurse them back to health. Most of the time no one really paid attention because her parents were too busy fighting and calling the police on each other. So Rachel could spend hours playing "hospital" with her dolls, taking care of sick animals, and keeping herself company. As she grew older, wounded people were attracted to her and her circle of friends looked more like a caseload. It was natural for Rachel to go to college to be a therapist so she could continue her vicarious nurturing. Rachel met her husband while volunteering at the Veteran's Center when one of the men on the psychiatric ward started paying attention to her and convinced her that, with her love, he would stay sober.

Neglect can take the form of ignoring or not seeing another's humanness. By withholding care, nurturing and attention we shut down the relational behaviors that reflect attunement and connection. Neglect can be particularly difficult to treat because there is no easy behavior to on which to pin wounded feelings. Clients are left feeling as though they have too many needs to meet. They grow mistrustful of deep connection. (Avoidant/dismissive style)

Arlene's mom had always struggled with parenting, becoming over-whelmed by simple dilemmas such as a broken garbage disposal or an overdue bill. Arlene was ashamed of her mom because other people's mothers seemed "more adult" while her mom seemed like such a mess. Arlene's dad was rarely home and Arlene was often left with the task of putting her mom back together again after the latest crisis. Arlene de-spised her mother's weakness and had no tolerance for signs of weak-ness in herself. In fact, whenever she felt afraid or confused she would simply tell herself to "stop whining" and "don't be such a half-wit." As an adult, Arleen would tell you she is never afraid. She simply does the next thing in front of her and she has no patience for people who whine and act pathetic and needy.

Abuse vs. Victimization

Emotional, physical and psychological abuse is present all too of-ten in families that contain under-functioning adults and trauma. Abuse is part of the impulsivity that results in families where feel-ings are acted out rather than talked out. The other side of abuse is victimization. This is a dynamic in which the abused child, having felt helpless and victimized, ultimately becomes the abusing parent. They act out their childhood pain by passing it on just as they expe-rienced it, rather than identifying and feeling their own helplessness and rage at being a victim of abuse. This is how traumatic and ad-diction fostering familial patterns of relating become multigenera-tional (transmitted from one generation to the next).

Tamara had watched the violence between her parents all her life until she found a way to move out at 16 years old and move in with her older brother. As she heard her mother cry out and saw her bruises Tamara began to feel contempt for her mother, encouraging her to just "leave the bastard." Her mother never did leave him. Tamara is very sure that she would never put up with anybody's "shit" the way her mother did. She is very alert to signs that she is being disrespected or abused. In fact, the minute anyone she is dating begins to "tell me what to do," Tamara is quick to tell him about himself. If that means slapping or punching him in the chest to "get his attention" then that's what has to be done. Her motto is "stop the bastard in his tracks before he hurts me." If you told Tamara she was violent herself, she would deny it or state that she was only acting in self-defense.

Triangulation

A triangle is a three-person relationship system. It is considered the building block or "molecule" of larger emotional systems because a triangle is the smallest stable relationship system. A two-person system is unstable because it tolerates little tension before involving a third person or even an outside focus such as alcohol or work. A triangle can contain much more tension without involving another person because the tension can shift around the three relationships. If the tension is too high for one triangle to contain, it spreads to a series of "interlocking" triangles.

Spreading the tension can stabilize a system, but nothing gets resolved. People's actions in a triangle reflect several things: efforts to maintain emotional attachments to important others, reactions to too high intensity in the attachments, and taking sides in the conflicts of others.

Denise has watched her parents fight for years over control in their marriage. Her parents seem to be incapable of operating as a team. They are too competitive and distrusting of each other's motives to create a positive plan of action. She is convinced that the only reason they did not divorce was fear of how vicious the other might be in a custody fight! However, Denise has battled a rare blood disorder her whole life. Periodically she becomes very ill and needs to be hospitalized for a few weeks to stabilize her blood count. It was during these periods that her parents would present a united front, both equally invested in their love for Denise. An adult now, Denise visits her parents from time to time but finds if they start to fight over Thanksgiving dinner she begins to feel unwell. It puzzles her because she normally takes good care of herself and is proactive in her own medical care. Yet for some reason when she is with her parents she is prone to illness and, for that brief period of time, the fighting stops.

The idea that a triangle is more stable than a dyad seems paradoxical because a triangle creates an "odd man out," a very difficult position for individuals to tolerate. Anxiety generated by anticipating or being the odd one out is a potent force in triangles (creates an anxious response to potential broken attachments). The patterns in a triangle change with increasing tension. In calm periods, two people are comfortably close "insiders" and the third person is an uncomfortable "outsider." The insiders actively exclude the outsider and the outsider works to get closer with one of them.

Jennifer is very aware that her sister Laura is her mother's favorite. In fact her mother will admit she prefers Laura's company since she was an easier child. They have more in common than Jennifer and her mother have in common. When Jennifer visits her family she always feels lonely and is unsure about her place in the family. She often jokes that she was adopted.

However, Jennifer's father has recently been showing cognitive problems. He has trouble finding his words, his memory is poor and he is afraid to make decisions. It appears to Jennifer that the problem requires a neurological exam but the medical world scares her parents. Jennifer is a nursing instructor and far more comfortable with the language. As a result, Jennifer's mother is calling Jennifer more and her sister Laura is beginning to show signs of irritability and is picking fights with Jennifer over trivial issues. In talking to her sponsor, Jennifer realizes that Laura is afraid of losing her position as the favorite and may even be jealous of Jennifer's new contact with their mother.

At moderate levels of tension, triangles usually have one side in conflict and two sides in harmony. The conflict is not inherent in the relationships but reflects the overall functioning of the triangle. At a high level of tension, the outside position becomes the most desirable. If severe conflict erupts between the insiders, one insider opts for the outside position by getting the current outsider fighting with the other insider (an avoidant/dismissive attachment maneuver). If the avoidant insider is successful, he gains the more comfortable position of watching the other two people fight. When the tension and conflict subsides, the outsider (avoidant person) will try to regain an inside position.

Gloria has three children, all of whom would diagnose her as "narcissistic." Their father has survived the long marriage by essentially remaining in the background and saying "yes dear" a great deal. His sons hate this about him, wishing he had a spine. When the oldest son, John, decided to marry a non-Catholic, Gloria went ballistic. She was inconsolable. As the fighting escalated between John and Gloria over that "bimbo," his father became almost completely invisible waiting for the fray to settle down. Once the intensity began to recede, John's father could safely step in to assume the role of "comforter."

Triangles contribute significantly to the development of clinical problems. Getting pushed from an inside to an outside position can trigger a depression or perhaps even a physical illness. Two parents intensely focusing on what is wrong with a child can trigger serious rebellion in the child.

Kevin is the "black sheep" of the family, always the center of family gossip. Kevin's twin, Jaime, did well in school, was a boy scout, and had a nice girlfriend. He played by all the rules. Unfortunately his success made him invisible and the lack of family attention left him feeling alone. Kevin, on the other hand, was a constant screw up. Drugs, continuation high school, multiple rehabs... Kevin's antics served as a lightening rod absorbing most of the family's attention. Increasingly Jaime dreaded family occasions and would find "acceptable" reasons to avoid participating.

Kevin seemed to be on a good streak lately. He'd discharged probation for the first time in 6 years, he was attending school and seemed to be clean and sober. Jaime noticed how instead of the family healing they began to turn their attention to why he, Jaime, was avoiding the family. He started getting more pressured phone calls from his mom, guilting him about his absence on Easter. He started catching disappointed looks from his father when he would visit. Jaime was truly annoyed and puzzled.

The communication solution for stability in the family is direct communication. Relationships are maintained and conflicts are addressed between the two people involved. This means there needs to be emotional trust between family members that creates the safety to be honest with each other, even when it is uncomfortable. Ultimately, we have to trust our attachment to take emotional risks.

Emotional Cut-off

The concept of emotional cutoff describes people managing their unresolved emotional issues with parents, siblings and other family members by reducing or totally cutting off emotional contact with them. Emotional contact can be reduced by people moving away from their families and rarely going home, or it can be reduced by people staying in physical contact with their families but avoiding sensitive issues. Relationships may look "better" if people cutoff to manage them, but the problems are still there and not resolved.

When people cut off family members to reduce the tensions of interactions, they risk making their new relationships too important. For example, the more a man cuts off from his family of origin, the more he looks to his spouse, children and friends to meet his needs. This makes him vulnerable to pressuring them to be certain ways for him, or trying too hard to meet their expectations of him out of fear of losing the relationship. The new relationships are typically smooth at first but the same patterns people are trying to escape eventually reemerge and generate tension. Also, the people who are cut off may try to stabilize their own intimate relationships by creating substitute "families" with social and work relationships.

Susan found her father's criminal history embarrassing and she had never introduced a boyfriend to the family. In fact, when she would meet new people she would lie about her family, describing them as middle class and saying that her father had been a teacher. Susan worked very hard to educate herself and distance herself from the "trailer park mentality" she grew up with. When Susan met her future husband, Dan, she not only told him the revised family history but added that both parents were deceased so she could avoid awkward conversations about family visits. This was more comfortable for her and she wasn't worried since she lived 3000 miles away from her mill town.

While Dan adored Susan, he often felt pressured by her upscale desires or what he called "pretentious" need to keep up with the Joneses. He couldn't understand why he couldn't wear his old T-shirts when they went shopping and why she couldn't stand for him to have steel-toed boots. She was very adamant about their white-collar status as a couple and a family. He honestly found it a bit embarrassing when Susan would "put on airs" while visiting his modest, middle class family. When they wanted to watch wrestling she could barely be polite and would practically run out of the room. Dan would just shake his head.

An unresolved attachment can take many forms. For example,

1. a person feels more like a child when he is home and looks to his parents to make decisions for him that he can make for himself, or

2. a person feels guilty when he is in more contact with his parents and that he must solve their conflicts or distresses, or

3. a person feels enraged that his parents do not seem to understand or approve of him.

An unresolved attachment relates to the immaturity of both the parents and the adult child, but people typically blame themselves or others for the problems.

People often look forward to going home, hoping things will be different this time, but the old interactions usually surface within hours. It may take the form of surface harmony with powerful emotional undercurrents or it may deteriorate into shouting matches and hysterics. Both the person and his family may feel exhausted even after a brief visit. It may be easier for the parents if an adult child keeps his distance. The family gets so anxious and reactive when he is home that they are relieved when he leaves. The siblings of a highly cutoff member often get furious at him when he is home and blame him for upsetting the parents. People do not want it to be this way, but the sensitivities of all parties are a barrier to comfortable contact.

Barbara had been looking forward to seeing her sisters, nieces, nephews and Uncle Gary for the last month. She had missed the family, and tried not to think too much about the fact that her mother would be at the event as well. It was her niece's high school graduation (the first one) and everyone was so excited. When Barbara arrived she was thrilled to be surrounded by so many people she loved and in her enthusiasm even genuinely hugged her mother. Maybe it would be different "this time."

As the group started to assemble for the drive over to the high school, Barbara's mom suggested family photos. Truly, it was not the best time to do this and would potentially make them late. The sisters looked at each other, and with a well-practiced cue Barbara used a condescending tone to point out the problem with this idea, and her mother looked hurt. Barbara found herself rolling her eyes at her sisters, indicating, "There goes Mom again" completely oblivious to her role in speaking to her mother like a 15 year old.

This is a puzzling phenomenon many of us have experienced. For example, we are a 36 year old woman as we drive to our parent's house for Thanksgiving. However, with 30 minutes of arrival, we find ourselves adopting the tone and mannerisms we used when we were 13 years old! Friends who may be joining us are shocked by our immature behavior when we "slam" the door to the bathroom to emphasize a point we are making to a family member.

CHAPTER FOUR

A FEW MORE NOTES ABOUT DEVELOPMENTAL TASK COMPLETION OVER THE LIFESPAN

My premise for this text was that early attachment disruption lays the developmental foundation for anxious/ambivalent and avoidant/dismissive codependency. Therefore I have devoted the majority of my research focus to this crucial developmental task. However, Erik Erikson pointed out that development happens throughout the life span, and the Weinhold's suggested in The Codependency Trap (20) that understanding our developmental "gaps" was key to long-term resolution of codependency. I have seen this to be true in my work with recovering clients. I am including an exploration of Erik Erikson's developmental stages, asking you to make the connections between codependent behaviors and developmental interruption.

Development is interrupted by trauma, chronic stress and excessive needs of caregivers. *Why* we have developmental holes is not as important as the fact that the holes are present, and we need to take steps to fill in the gaps where they occur. I often have clients complete a developmental time-line and take a look at areas, or tasks, in which they can see interruptions, and then link them to codependency and addiction. You may find this exercise helpful as well.

Erikson's stages of psychosocial development outline eight stages through which a healthily developing human should pass from infancy to late adulthood. In each stage the person confronts, and hopefully masters, new challenges. Each stage builds on the successful completion of earlier stages. The challenges of stages not successfully completed may be expected to reappear as problems in the future.

Hope: Trust vs. Mistrust (Infants, 0 to 1 year)

- Psychosocial Crisis: Trust vs. Mistrust
- Virtue: Hope

Erikson's first stage centers around the infant's basic needs being met by the parents. The infant depends on the parents, especially the mother, for food, sustenance and comfort. The child's relative understanding of world and society come from the parents and their interaction with the child. If the parents expose the child to warmth, regularity and dependable affection, the infant's view of the world will be one of trust. Should the parents fail to provide a secure environment or not meet the child's basic needs a sense of mistrust will result. *According to Erik Erikson, the major developmental task in infancy is to learn whether or not other people, especially primary caregivers, regularly satisfy basic needs.* If caregivers are consistent sources of food, comfort and affection the infant learns trust (others are dependable and reliable). If caregivers are neglectful, or perhaps even abusive, the infant instead learns mistrust (the world is in an undependable, unpredictable and possibly dangerous place).

Will: Autonomy vs. Shame & Doubt (Toddlers, 2 to 3 years)

- Psychosocial Crisis: Autonomy vs. Shame & Doubt
- Main Question: "Can I do things myself or must I always rely on others?"
- Virtue: Will

As the child gains control over eliminative functions and motor abilities, they begin to explore their surroundings. The parents still provide a strong base of security from which the child can venture out to assert their will. The parents' patience and encouragement help foster autonomy in the child. Highly restrictive parents, however, are more likely to instill a sense of doubt and reluctance to attempt new challenges.

As they gain increased muscular coordination and mobility, toddlers become capable of satisfying some of their own needs. They begin to feed themselves, wash and dress themselves and use the bathroom. *If caregivers encourage self-sufficient behavior, toddlers develop a sense of autonomy, a sense of being able to handle many problems on their own.* But if caregivers demand too much too soon, refuse to let children perform tasks of which they are capable or ridicule early attempts at self-sufficiency, children may instead develop shame and doubt about their ability to handle problems.

Purpose: Initiative vs. Guilt (Preschool, 4 to 6 years)

- Psychosocial Crisis: Initiative vs. Guilt
- Main Question: "Am I good or am I bad?"
- Virtue: Purpose
- Related Elements in Society: ideal prototypes/roles

Initiative adds the quality of undertaking, planning and attacking a task for the sake of being active and on the move. The child is learning to master the world around him, learning basic skills and principles of physics. Things fall down, not up. Round things roll. He learns how to zip and tie, count and speak with ease. At this stage, the child wants to begin and complete his own actions for a purpose. Guilt is a confusing new emotion. He may feel guilty over things that logically should not cause guilt. He may feel guilt when his initiative does not produce desired results.

The development of courage and independence are what set preschoolers, ages three to six years, apart from other age groups. Young children in this category face the challenge of initiative versus guilt. As described in Bee and Boyd (22), the child during this stage faces the complexities of planning and developing a sense of judgment. During this stage, the child learns to take initiative and prepare for leadership and goal achievement roles. Activities sought out by a child in this stage may include risk-taking behaviors, such as crossing a street alone or riding a bike without a helmet; both examples involving self-limits. Within instances requiring initiative, the child may also develop negative behaviors. These behaviors are a result of the child developing a sense of frustration for not being able to achieve a goal as planned and may engage in behaviors that seem aggressive, ruthless or overly assertive to parents.

Aggressive behaviors such as throwing objects, hitting or yelling are examples of observable behaviors during this stage. Preschoolers are increasingly able to accomplish tasks on their own and with this growing independence comes many choices about activities to be pursued. Sometimes children take on projects they can readily accomplish, but at other times they undertake projects that are beyond their capabilities or that interfere with other people's plans and activities. *If parents and preschool teachers encourage and support children's efforts, while also helping them make realistic and appropriate choices, children develop initiative, independence in planning and undertaking activities.* But if adults discourage the pursuit of independent activities or dismiss them as silly and bothersome, children develop guilt about their needs and desires.

Competence: Industry vs. Inferiority (Childhood, 7 to 12 years)
- Psychosocial Crisis: Industry vs. Inferiority
- Main Question: "Am I successful or worthless?"
- Virtue: Competence
- Related Elements in Society: division of labor

The aim to bring a productive situation to completion gradually supersedes the whims and wishes of play.

"Children at this age are becoming more aware of themselves as individuals." They work hard at "being responsible, being good and doing it right." They are now more reasonable and able to share and cooperate. Allen and Marotz (23) also list some perceptual cognitive developmental traits specific for this age group: Children understand the concepts of space and time in more logical and practical ways. They are beginning to grasp calendar time and gain a better understanding of cause and effect. At this stage, children are eager to learn and accomplish more complex skills: reading, writing and telling time. They also get to form moral values, recognize cultural and individual differences and are able to manage most of their personal needs and grooming with minimal assistance (24). At this stage, children might express their independence by being disobedient, using back talk and being rebellious.

Erikson viewed the elementary school years as critical for the development of self-confidence. Ideally, elementary school provides many opportunities for children to achieve the recognition of teachers, parents and peers by producing things — drawing pictures, solving addition problems, writing sentences and so on. *If children are encouraged to make and do things and are then praised for their accomplishments, they begin to demonstrate industry by being diligent, persevering at tasks until completed and putting work before pleasure.* If children are instead ridiculed or punished for their efforts or if they find they are incapable of meeting their teachers' and/or parents' expectations, they develop feelings of inferiority about their capabilities.

Fidelity: Identity vs. Role Confusion (Adolescents, 13 to 19 years)

- Psychosocial Crisis: Identity vs. Role Confusion
- Main Question: "Who am I and where am I going?"
- Ego quality: Fidelity
- Related Elements in Society: ideology

The adolescent is newly concerned with how they appear to others. Superego identity is the accrued confidence that the outer sameness and continuity prepared in the future are matched by the sameness and continuity of one's meaning for oneself, as evidenced in the promise of a career. The ability to settle on a school or occupational identity is pleasant. In later stages of Adolescence, the child develops a sense of sexual identity.

As they make the transition from childhood to adulthood, adolescents ponder the roles they will play in the adult world. Initially, they are apt to experience some role confusion - mixed ideas and feelings about the specific ways in which they will fit into society - and may experiment with a variety of behaviors and activities (e.g. tinkering with cars, baby-sitting for neighbors, affiliating with certain political or religious groups). *Eventually, Erikson proposed most adolescents achieve a sense of identity regarding who they are and where their lives are headed.*

Erikson is credited with coining the term "Identity Crisis." Each stage that came before and that follows has its own 'crisis', but even more so now, for this marks the transition from childhood to adulthood. This passage is necessary because "Throughout infancy and childhood, a person forms many identifications. But the need for identity in youth is not met by these." *This turning point in human development seems to be the reconciliation between the person one has come to be and the person society expects one to become.* This emerging sense of self will be established by 'forging' past experiences with anticipations of the future. In relation to the eight life stages as a whole, the fifth stage corresponds to the crossroads.

What is unique about the stage of Identity is that it is a special sort of synthesis of earlier stages and a special sort of anticipation of later ones. Youth has a certain unique quality in a person's life; it is a bridge between childhood and adulthood. Youth is a time of radical change — the body changes accompanying puberty, the ability of the mind to search one's own intentions and the intentions of others, the suddenly sharpened awareness of societal roles for later life.

Adolescents are confronted by the need to re-establish [boundaries] for themselves and to do this in the face of an often potentially hostile world. This is often challenging since commitments are being asked for before particular identity roles have formed. At this point, one is in a state of identity confusion but society normally makes allowances for youth to find themselves, and this state is called "the moratorium."

The problem of adolescence is one of role confusion — a reluctance to commit which may haunt a person into his mature years. *Given the right conditions though, what may emerge is a firm sense of identity, on emotional and deep awareness of who he or she is. Erikson believes these right conditions are essentially having enough space and time, and a psychological moratorium when a person can freely experiment and explore.*

As in other stages, bio-psycho-social forces are at work. No matter how one is raised, one's personal ideologies are now chosen. Often this leads to conflict with adults over religious and political orientations. Another area where teenagers are deciding for themselves is career choice, and frequently parents want to have a decisive say in that role. If society is too insistent the teenager will acquiesce to external wishes, effectively undermining experimentation and, consequently, true self-discovery. Once someone settles on a worldview and vocation, will he or she be able to integrate this aspect of self-definition into a diverse society? According to Erikson, when an adolescent has balanced both perspectives of "What have I got?" and "What am I going to do with it?" he or she has established their identity.

Dependent on this stage is the ego quality of *fidelity – the ability to sustain loyalties freely pledged in spite of the inevitable contradictions and confusions of value systems.*

Given that the next stage (Intimacy) is often characterized by marriage, many are tempted to cap off the fifth stage at 20 years of age. However, these age ranges are actually quite fluid, especially for the achievement of identity. It may take many years to become grounded, to identify the object of one's fidelity and to feel that one has "come of age." In the biographies *Young Man Luther* and *Gandhi's Truth*, Erikson determined that their crises ended at ages 25 and 30, respectively.

Erikson does note that the time of identity crisis for persons of genius is frequently prolonged. He further notes that in our industrial society, identity formation tends to be long, because it takes us so long to gain the skills needed for adulthood's tasks in our technological world. So… we do not have an exact time span in which to find ourselves. It doesn't happen automatically at eighteen or at twenty-one. A *very* approximate rule of thumb for our society would put the end somewhere in one's twenties.

Love: Intimacy vs. Isolation (Young Adults, 20 to 34 years)

- Psychosocial Crisis: Intimacy vs. Isolation
- Main Question: "Am I loved and wanted?" or "Shall I share my life with someone or live alone?"
- Virtue: Love
- Related Elements in Society: patterns of cooperation (often marriage)

Body and ego must master organ modes (and other nuclear conflicts) in order to face the fear of ego loss in situations that call for self-abandonment. Avoiding these experiences leads to openness and self-absorption.

The Intimacy vs. Isolation conflict is emphasized around the ages of 20 to 34. At the start of this stage, identity vs. role confusion is coming to an end and it still lingers at the foundation of the stage. Young adults are still eager to blend their identities with friends. They want to fit in. Erikson believes we are sometimes isolated due to fear of intimacy. We are afraid of rejections such as being turned down or partners breaking up with us. We are familiar with pain, and to some of us, rejection is painful; our egos cannot bear the pain. Erikson also argues that "Intimacy has a counterpart: Distantiation: *the readiness to isolate and if necessary, to destroy those forces and people whose essence seems dangerous to our own, and whose territory seems to encroach on the extent of one's intimate relations*" (25).

Once people have established their identities, they are ready to make long-term commitments to others. They become capable of forming intimate, reciprocal relationships (e.g. close friendships or marriage) and willingly make the sacrifices and compromises that such relationships require. If people cannot form these intimate relationships (perhaps because of their own needs) a sense of isolation may result.

Care: Generativity vs. Stagnation (Middle Adulthood, 35 to 65 years)

- Psychosocial Crisis: Generativity vs. Stagnation

- Main Question: "Will I produce something of real value?"
- Virtue: Care
- Related Elements in Society: parenting, educating or other productive social involvement

Generativity is the concern of establishing and guiding the next generation. Socially-valued work and disciplines are expressions of generativity. Simply having or wanting children does not, in and of itself, achieve generativity.

During middle age the primary developmental task is one of contributing to society and helping to guide future generations. When a person makes a contribution during this period, perhaps by raising a family or working toward the betterment of society, a sense of generativity (productivity and accomplishment) results. In contrast, a person who is self-centered and unable or unwilling to help society move forward develops a feeling of stagnation, a dissatisfaction with their relative lack of productivity.

Central tasks of Middle Adulthood

- Express love through more than sexual contacts.
- Maintain healthy life patterns.
- Develop a sense of unity with mate.
- Help growing and grown children to be responsible adults.
- Relinquish central role in lives of grown children.
- Accept children's mates and friends.
- Create a comfortable home.
- Be proud of accomplishments of self and mate/spouse.
- Reverse roles with aging parents.
- Achieve mature, civic and social responsibility.
- Adjust to physical changes of middle age.
- Use leisure time creatively.
- Love for others.

Wisdom: Ego Integrity vs. Despair (Seniors, 65 years onwards)

- Psychosocial Crisis: Ego Integrity vs. Despair
- Main Question: "Have I lived a full life?"
- Virtue: Wisdom

As we grow older and become senior citizens we tend to slow down our productivity and explore life as a retired person. It is during this time that we contemplate our accomplishments and are able to develop integrity if we see ourselves as leading a successful life. If we see our life as unproductive or feel that we did not accomplish our life goals, we become dissatisfied with life and develop despair, often leading to depression and hopelessness.

The final developmental task is retrospection: people look back on their lives and accomplishments. They develop feelings of content-ment and integrity if they believe that they have led a happy, produc-tive life. They may develop a sense of despair if they look back on a life of disappointments and unachieved goals.

Afraid to Let Go

PART TWO

Our anxiety-based responses to life can include over-reactivity, image management, unrealistic beliefs about our limits, and attempts to control the reality of others to the point where we lose our boundaries, self-esteem, and even our own reality.

CHAPTER FIVE

ANXIOUS/AMBIVALENT CODEPENDENT PATTERNS

If I am an anxious codependent parent, then my lack of trust in my child's love and attachment to me will appear in several ways:

Symptom One: Lack of Attunement with Self

Anxious/ambivalent attached adults struggle when faced with unstructured time. This is because we:

- had our solitude repeatedly interrupted by the demanding needs of our caregiver
- constantly attempt to monitor threats to attachment, and
- were not allowed time to disengage from caretaking

So we became prematurely and compulsively attuned to the demands of others.

Avoiding awareness of our own reality is often an attempt to deny thoughts, desires or intentions that we feel will threaten or contradict the needs of those with whom we feel strong attachment. We instinctively hide feelings and thoughts we assume to be threatening to other people (and might cause them to leave us).

When we don't trust other people's attachment to us we develop an absence of self, or in Peter Fonagy's words "an openness to colonization" by the mental states of other important people in our lives. Our reality becomes defined by our ability to accurately mirror the reality those around us wish us to have.

Jim and Diane had been divorced for the last ten years, with rare but in high conflict exchanges when they were forced to speak regarding

their now adult son, Terry. Terry is 24 years old, and struggling to find his direction in life. He has a history of not completing coursework or prematurely quitting jobs, and it was Diane's position that he just needed time to "find himself." When Jim pressured her to "set some boundaries" with Terry, she would try but found his silent treatment and avoidance of her so painful that she would soon relent on limits she set with him. While Jim clearly thought Terry's lack of progress in life was connected to his marijuana use and alcohol intake, Diane patiently sat through long conversations with Terry as he read the latest report on the internet justifying the harmlessness of marijuana and dismissing her own ideas. In her mind, the priority was to keep the lines of communication open and not threaten the relationship by taking a hard line. She had watched Terry distance himself from his father as Jim grew more vocal about Terry's lack of progress in life, and she was afraid this could happen if she pressured the issue too much.

While it may be obvious to the reader that Terry is using emotional blackmail with his mother, and it has been effective. It is also possible to have empathy for her if you have been on the receiving end of feeling "shut out" by someone you care for a great deal who is angry. It is painful to be "dismissed" and disregarded, and for many of us, conflict is far more preferred. The rationale: At least we're talking!

James started using crack when he was 20 years old when his first cousin introduced him to it. He had 2½ years of college, majoring in psychology. After many local jail sentences, he was eventually sent to federal prison. He served 26 months for selling to an undercover cop. He is not a dealer per se, wanted to use crack so he sold it to get it.

Over the years his mother, Susan, had been a faithful member of Al-Anon, in hope that one day James would work his program. She had many sleepless nights over the years, and even now can't fully accept what has happened despite his criminal justice history. Susan honestly thought she would somehow be "exempt" from his behavior.

When James got out of federal prison for 3 months, he lived with his girl friend and his 2 children. When Susan went on a 14 day cruise, she returned to find her house had been broken into and several items were missing from her shed. She was very, very angry and surprised. She went to the local pawn shops, found her stolen items and had him arrested. It still feels surreal to her, though everyone in the family had been cautioning her for years.

One of the more troubling aspects for parents who abandon themselves is their denial of the new potential criminality of their adult children. Prior to addiction, you may have trusted your adult child to house-sit, or take care of your pets while you traveled. Prior to addiction, you were comfortable with your adult child's friends, and welcomed them freely in your home whether or not you were present. In fact, to do anything else my never have entered your mind.

However, the reality of your vulnerability to their increasingly criminal lifestyle can become a rude awakening unless you are willing to acknowledge their changing behaviors and social world.

Secure attachment requires the early acquisition and acceptance of a self with independent boundaries, a sense that I am differentiated from you. Children taught to respect parental needs to the exclusion of their own developmental needs will often continue to play out this working mode of conditional attachment throughout their life. "You will attach to me as long as I meet your needs."

Diane and Susan clearly have adopted this model, fully believing a permanent rift is possible with their sons if they acknowledge the reality of who they have become in the addiction. They are willing to abdicate their own concerns, and even their safety in favor of protecting their connection. In extreme cases this becomes the defense of depersonalization – the sense of estrangement from (or feeling of unreality about) the bodily or mental self. We lack an internal observer, and often cannot recognize ourselves physically, emotionally, intellectually or spiritually. It's as though we have to walk around the world asking others, "Do I look like her?" "Do I sound like him?"

When we lack an accurate internal observer we cannot self-correct and identify our blind spots. We are unable to establish effective boundaries either internally (our thoughts or feelings) or externally (our physical self and our possessions). We are vulnerable to subtle and constant merging with those around us as we take on their emotions and their thoughts. We are vulnerable to the energetic influence of others. Our moods can be impacted and sharply shifted by changes in the people around us. Much like an invisible vapor, we "take in" their energy without being aware we are doing so.

Have you ever felt that a part of you wanted to do something while another part of you did not? Or, you really want to kick a habit of some sort but no matter what you do it feels like some part of you won't let you? Or have you ever found yourself reacting to someone in a surprising way, possibly overreacting to something…just watching yourself react and not being able to stop…and feeling remorse or embarrassment afterwards?

In the current neuroscience circles exploring how the brain and mind work, this may be called a frozen or "stuck" neural network. The bottom line here is that most of us have some part, or parts, of self that act or react depending on the particular situation. There is nothing inherently wrong with this…it's natural as we learn to compartmentalize our experience and live our lives. For instance, we change our roles and how we act when we go to work versus when we are at home with our families. We act differently with a store clerk versus a loved one. These are all healthy shifts we make depending on the part of us we need at any given time or in any given situation. For the most part, these are conscious and mindful ways of being and essential to living.

Sometimes, though, these processes begin to act outside of a conscious and/or mindful way of being. When someone cuts you off in traffic and you go into rage rather than annoyance…that is not a conscious or mindful reaction. When your boss calls you into the office and you automatically ask, "What did I do wrong?" and begin to feel like you're about 10 years old…that's not conscious and mindful. When your significant other pays attention to another person and you feel like crying or withdrawing into yourself or you want to leave them to protect yourself…that is not a conscious or mindful reaction.

Our lack of boundaries can be painfully obvious to everyone but us; and since we are so disconnected from our actual agendas, needs, and wants we can feel truly puzzled when someone comments about what they perceive to be our growing lack of self.

Having our emotions acknowledged accurately teaches us an emotional vocabulary we can use to acknowledge and share our emotional reality with others. When we grow up having to monitor and accurately read the emotions of caregivers rather than ourselves, our internal world remains a mystery to us. In fact, our internal world seems "beside the point." This also makes us clueless about our external world since we are oblivious how we effect others.

This is a primary contributor to my own ridiculousness, often barreling through the world completely unaware of the trail I leave behind me unless someone brings it to my attention.

Symptom Two: Lack of attunement with others

Frequently, anxiously attached codependents have not developed an understanding of other people's thoughts and emotions. We can lack empathy for feelings we don't understand. We have difficulty guessing and predicting other people's plans, intentions and motives, despite the fact that we are always monitoring them to figure out how we should act!

Because our caregivers were not emotionally attuned to our developing emotional reality, we never developed a cognitive or emotional "reflective capacity." Since we never had our internal world recognized or mirrored back to us we never learned to pay attention to our own emotional reality. We can't recognize our own feelings nor can we recognize the feelings of others. We are frequently confused by (or oblivious to) emotional worlds of others.

This is a puzzling aspect of Codependency because on the surface we seem so focused on the needs of others. We expend enormous energy anticipating and meeting the needs of those around us. However, we are usually responding to our PERCEPTIONS of the needs of those we love, not their actual needs. Quite often we don't even ask the people we're "caring for" about their needs and preferences. This explains the disconnect between our giving and their apparent lack of "gratitude" for our heroic efforts on their behalf!

Laura, the oldest child of divorced parents had been a single mother of three for the last fifteen years, choosing to forego another committed relationship after the death of her husband because she felt this was best for her children. She could sense their anxiety and resistance when tried to have a man come to the house, and would soon terminate the new relationship to stay focused on meeting the children's needs. As a result the children always carried a vague sense of guilt due to Laura's "sacrifice" for their sake. They had seen her loneliness over the years, and watched her struggle financially as they grew older yet knew that they "came first." If she had asked them, they would have enjoyed having a Dad as they grew older. But she never asked, interpreting their early resistance as a permanent position.

Laura's oldest daughter, Audrey, and been enrolled in two separate Outpatient addiction programs. She had completed a program when she was 15 years old, abusing marijuana and prescription medications, and was completing her second treatment program at 23 years old for abuse of Oxycontin and alcohol. Laura had been adamant with the treatment team that her daughter "must" return to her husband of two years who was clean and sober, had a good job, and was a good man. She felt strongly that her daughter's sobriety depended on this marriage, and offered to pay for as much couple's therapy as they needed to "make the marriage work." From Laura's perspective, her daughter Audrey was "lucky" that such a good man was willing to stay with her after all she had "put him through", and just the thought of a divorce made her feel sick.

Laura is completely unaware of her effect of her "sacrifice" and demands on those around her, truly believing that she is doing what is in their best interest, She is oblivious to how much she is acting her out her own terror of abandonment, having been suddenly widowed with three children and having her father disappear after her parents divorced. If asked, she would most likely not see the connection, keeping her focus on protecting her child from the "disaster" of being alone in the world the way Laura had been. Laura is oblivious to the guilt and obligation her daughter Audrey feels towards her, and her need to take alcohol and drugs to numb her unhappiness in a marriage she chose because her mother felt it was a good choice.

As anxiously attached Codependents, we are completely disconnected from our own internal experience which means we are unable to read the internal experience of others. Despite our hyper-vigilant focus on the changing emotional landscape of those around us, we cannot correctly interpret their feelings. In fact we usually suspect their emotional changes are somehow prompted by our actions, our inadequacy or our failing. *It is truly amazing how we place ourselves so grandly into the reality of others, yet we feel so insignificant ourselves!*

Pia Mellody, in Facing Codependence, (26) also references this reality distortion. She points out how we sometimes confuse our needs and wants, incorrectly interpreting the problem or applying an incorrect solution. For example, I need a hug but I buy a blouse. The developmental implications of the inability to effectively self-soothe are tremendous. Our inability to connect "the problem" with an appropriate "solution" leads us to various addictions in an attempt to relieve the discomfort and anxiety pervading our relationships.

We are uncomfortable in our own skin yet we continually misattribute the source of this discomfort. Deep down, many of us carry a pervasive belief that we are "too broken" to handle or regulate our emotions. We genuinely believe if we ever have to feel the full impact of our emotions, we will die.

Symptom Three: Distrusting the Attachment of Others to the Codependent

Individuals who exhibit the anxious/ambivalent style:

- feel others are reluctant to get as close to them as they would like.

- worry their partners do not really love them or do not want to stay with them.

- want their partners to get very close to them while *not offering the same level of disclosure and intimacy.*

Others may perceive this as controlling or even "hostage" taking.

Similarly to the avoidant/dismissive attachment style, people with an anxious/ambivalent attachment style seek less intimacy from our partners and frequently suppress and hide our feelings, suspecting that our feelings and needs might be "overwhelming" or "too much" for our partners to handle.

Matthew and Carla were frantically researching treatment centers for their son, Andrew, who had recently overheard his boss express concerns about Andrew's poor work performance and hinting that it might be time to eliminate Andrew's position. Andrew, who was 34, had shared this with his parents the night before over four glasses of wine at dinner, railing about the politics of the office and making paranoid statements about his "man-hating" female boss. Matthew and Carla have watched this scenario play out in other work settings, and could see the writing on the wall. The last time Andrew was in this situation Matthew had consulted with his own HR department, and was advised that if Andrew asked for a leave to go into treatment, he would be protected by ADA and be qualified for a disability check while he was in treatment.

Matthew and Carla picked a program they felt would be acceptable to Andrew, and brought him to the treatment program without telling him in advance. This was their version of an intervention. After initial resistance and resentment, Andrew agreed to stay if he was provided

with detox medications, which he was given. At the first family group session it became readily apparent that while Matthew wanted full disclosure of Andrew's progress and thinking process, he was noticeably reluctant to discuss his own feelings about Andrew's drinking. Prior to admitting Andrew, Matthew had never discussed the impact of Andrew's alcoholism on him and his wife primarily because he felt Andrew couldn't "handle it" and he didn't want to make things "worse." If he was honest, he was pretty sure Andrew wasn't particularly interested in how Matthew was feeling.

It is evident that Matthew had concern about Andrew, so much so that he was willing to go outside his usual private boundary to consult with HR for guidance. Still, Andrew was shocked to find himself in a rehabilitation center. It is quite possible that Matthew had occasionally hinted at his concern, and obviously had confided in his wife Carla. But he did not trust his son with this level of intimacy and honesty.

Bob and Aimee had divorced when their only son, Jacob, was 9 years old. Bob was a prominent surgeon in the community and Jacob had been raised in an environment of opportunity and wealth from an early age. He had his own golf clubs, made to his height as he was growing up, and was usually considered "one of the guys" when he was with his father. As an adolescent, it was acceptable for him to drink with the adults, and at the age of 16, sometime drove Bob home because his Dad had too much to drink. This situation drove Aimee crazy with concern for Jacob, yet attempts to confront Bob on his behavior were rapidly dismissed by both Bob and Jacob as hysteria, and Jacob's excellent grades were "obvious" proof that there was not a problem.

By his sophomore year in college, Jacob was obviously struggling. He was not attending classes on time, if at all. He was taking W's to avoid getting F's. He picked up his first of several "drunk in public" charges which were rapidly taken care of by his father, though they resulted in conflict between them due to Jacob's "embarrassment" of Bob in the community. Jacob's last drunk charge was dismissed based on his willingness to attend an Outpatient program. Bob brought Jacob to the session obviously annoyed at the schedule interruption this caused for him.

Bob could not understand, after all he had given to "the boy", that "the boy" could be so irresponsible. Bob obviously felt betrayed by Jacob, interpreting his alcohol abuse as a personal rejection, and was resistant to any indications or awareness that he may have an alcohol problem himself. Bob voiced his concern that he was just an ATM for his son, and accused Jacob of planning to "get a free" ride all his life instead of thinking of a way to "give back" some of what he had so generously been given all these years. It was clear Bob felt that Jacob "owed" him something.

People who are anxious or preoccupied with attachment suspect that others don't value us as much as we value them, often because we are over-giving and others cannot match our participation level. So, when we notice the discrepancy between our giving levels, and the giving levels of others, we can develop resentments and interpret the imbalance as further proof that we are not "worthy" of being taken care of. It is proof of our foundational unloveability.

Our attempts to seek reassurance of our value and loveability can give us the appearance of neediness, with high levels of intensity due to emotional expressiveness and even impulsivity.

Anxiously attached Codependents frequently feel a strong need to "earn" the attachment of others. They distrust the idea that who they are will be enough. We over-extend, over-give, and seem to be always operating from a deficit position. It is as though we are "making up for" everything we are not. We notice other people do not seem to extend this much energy into their relationships and this is puzzling, because for us it's not optional. Over-achieving is "required" to secure attachments from people we love, though we never really trust the attachment because we believe it is based on what we do. If we slip up and fail to "do" our appointed role adequately, we could be replaced by someone who better meets the needs of our partners. It's a chronic stress to believe that you are always one mistake away from being abandoned.

Add to this our own conditional giving pattern, which fuels so much of our resentment and feelings of "victimization." We may be so completely unaware of our expectations of those we assist that our anger and resentment can catch us off guard. This is why our martyrdom is so hard on those around us. They know the price we are exacting, even when we are in denial about our own motives and expectations.

Sharon had been a stay-at-home Mom with a successful contractor husband who was frequently out of town to work with exclusive development sites as a consultant. Curtis, the middle of her three children, had always been a rambunctious child who struggled with his school work. However, he had been very successful socially, and was highly active with a wide range of friends. Sharon had grown up with her sisters and a single mother who worked three jobs to support the girls, so she had become self-sufficient and competent at a young age. Sharon had a strong sense of the "right thing to do" and felt very strongly that because she had the privilege of staying home with her children, she should give them everything her mother had not been able to give her. Sharon never missed a PTA meeting, Cub scouts, Brownies, Magazine Drives, Soccer game. . . Sharon prided herself on how "tuned in" she was with all three of her children and frequently pointed out that their communication was so strong that there were never any secrets.

Sharon had a tendency to be judgmental of parents who were not as available, and she was particularly secretly disapproving of the parents of Henry, her son's best friend. Sharon felt they were selfish to take cruises without the children at times, and was appalled that even though Henry's mother had Wednesday off from work, she would NOT go to every soccer game. Sharon felt sorry for Henry, and over the years tried to offer him the attention she felt he "should" have.

One afternoon, when Curtis was 21 and at work, Sharon received a call from Henry's mother who was phoning from the local hospital emergency room. Henry had called his mother because Curtis and Henry had called in sick at work to go up to lake to "party", and Curtis had so much to drink he was barely breathing. Fortunately, Henry knew CPR, called 911, and Curtis to the hospital in time.

Much to her horror, Sharon learned that this was not the first hospitalization for alcohol poisoning for her son. Curtis had sworn Henry to secrecy before, and brought in the mail so he could hide the hospital bills and his mother would not find out. Obviously they were delinquent because he did not make enough at work to fully cover them. The hospital was recommending a substance abuse treatment assessment at this point, and Sharon was faced with the fact that her "open" relationship with her children was not as open as she had believed. She felt betrayed, alone, resentful, and terrified. Curtis had confided in Henry's mother – the mother that she felt was "inadequate" while withholding from her, the "good mother."

Anxious codependents instinctually resent people who "get away" with acting poorly in a relationship and don't seem to lose the attachment. They have more permission and freedom in their relationships than the codependent. It is confusing and frustrating to work so hard ourselves only to see others "chosen" who have never (in our opinion) earned the continued attachments they enjoy.

The resentment is painful and overwhelming when we perceive that our attempts have failed to secure the loyalty and consistent responsiveness we have tried so hard to earn, yet others seem to just "get it" without effort. We blame ourselves, and sometimes feel victimized by others. This reminds me of the Karpman Drama Triangle, a classic description of the Codependent dilemma.

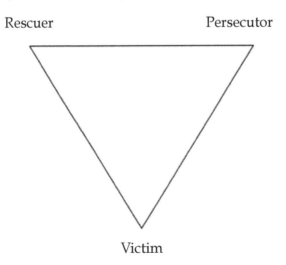

Rescuer   Persecutor

Victim

The anxiously attached codependent will notice that someone to whom they are attached has a "need." Without being asked for help or checking out the reality of the perceived need, the codependent will "offer" a solution to the need. This means we will describe the solution in detail and expect that they will apply the solution we have outlined.

If the person does not take our advice or acknowledge our "solution" we may begin to nag them, criticize them or even persecute them for failing to appreciate our efforts on their behalf.

Eventually, we will see ourselves as victimized by the person's lack of responsiveness to our advice or solution, and may even give ourselves permission to victimize them with tantrums and verbal abuse, while feeling victimized by the person we originally volunteered to help!

Ultimately, we are scared that our abusive behavior will destroy the original attachment, we will feel guilty and then attempt to secure the attachment by volunteering another form of assistance. And so the cycle continues.

Committed codependent's think at least once in their life, "If they would just do what I tell them, everything would be fine." In fact we repeat ourselves quite often. It is not to nag it's because if you don't do what we "suggest" we assume you didn't hear us. Because we know if you heard and understood what we were telling you, you would naturally CHOOSE to take our advice. But don't worry, we'll tell you again... and again, and again.

The painful part of this scenario is the pain we feel when you don't do what we suggest, or don't listen to us. We believe all we have to offer is what we can "do for you" or problems we can "solve," so when our offers are rejected, it goes into the, "See, I'm not worth it after all" pile. We are always finding evidence of this, and we unfortunately tend to gravitate towards people who will provide us with plenty of this kind of dismissive evidence.

Just as badly, we will martyr ourselves by suffering under the weight of a non-reciprocal relationship until some part of us bursts in protest. Suddenly we lose our mind, unleashing all manner of patronizing, name calling nastiness (even death threats) on the "deserving" jerk who has it coming after all we do for him or her! As the final insult rings across the room and we regain consciousness, we are horrified by what has come out of our mouth. After all, we LOVE these people! We quickly move into anxious terror, this time we have gone too far... this time we crossed the line and they will leave us. So, we hunker back down and the martyrdom begins again. It's a terrible cycle.

This escalation (or acting out behavior) is so young, isn't it? How old is it to have a tantrum, or tell Mommy "I hate you!" just to wound her? When I look at Codependent behavior I so often see the arrested emotional development that doesn't match our external competence. We are so accomplished in so many ways – so responsible and smart. How is it that such an articulate, accomplished woman is suddenly hurling words across the room, the way a four year old says, "I want a new Mommy!" From the outside, the powerlessness of this approach is obvious. There is no organized problem solving thought in this behavior. No personal responsibility for our choices.

Symptom Four: Escalation to protect attachment

As we learned in the developmental section, anxiously attached Codependents demonstrate the ability to maximize the attention they get from their partner, regardless of whether it is positive or negative (i.e., "I'd rather be screamed at than ignored").

Manipulation is used to keep the inattentive or inconsistent partner involved by alternating dramatic angry demands with needy dependence. When the partner is preoccupied and not paying attention, the anxious Codependent explodes in angry demands and behaviors that cannot be ignored.

The partner either reacts with hostility, punishing the codependent, or with sympathy, rewarding the manipulation. This cycle

Afraid to Let Go

can develop into patterns of responding to hostility with sweetness and dependency, and responding to sympathy with anger and new demands. The two are enmeshed together in a never-ending cycle of dissatisfaction.

Anxious/Ambivalent Codependents can be emotionally volatile adults who seek reassurance, but find only partial and temporary soothing from contact with the significant people in their lives. Their inability to self-soothe and regulate emotions creates a need for external calming solutions, including vulnerability to substance abuse to address our emotional distress.

Lisa and her daughter, Allison, had always been close. In fact they frequently traveled together to see Lisa's parents on the East Coast because her husband, Joe, was working. As Allison got older, she was Lisa's confidant when she would have any kind of conflict with Allison's father, and Lisa found just about everything Allison said or did interesting. She was the center of Lisa's world. Allison completed college without having established a serious relationship, and began spending increasing amounts of time with friends from work. Lisa noticed that she wasn't remembering their conversations well, and she often seemed to wake Allison up from a nap when she would call Allison to chat or complain about her father. It was taking Allison longer to return Lisa's calls, sometimes several days, and Lisa grew increasingly agitated and resentful. She began to lose sleep, lost her appetite, and her physician warned her about her rising blood pressure. One afternoon she became so agitated that she raced over to Allison's home, uninvited, and used the spare key she kept to feed her dog.

When Lisa entered the apartment it was squalid. It smelled, and there was dirty laundry piled in the living room. She bolted into Allison's bedroom and found her laying in bed, watching TV, with a fifth of Jack Daniels and a bottle of Xanax next to the bed. Allison was startled out of her stupor to see her, and as Lisa began to speak she felt her chest ache, arm go numb, and she passed out with a heart attack on the bed. Allison managed to find the phone in her bed covers, called 911, and got Lisa to the hospital. As she sat by her bedside, Lisa came to

and begged her to "never do this to me again". Allison agreed to enter alcohol and drug treatment.

Lisa is so blinded by her anxiety and fear of the growing distance with her daughter that she cannot see the potential outcome of creating such a distressing scene for both Allison and herself. When anxious codependents become triggered with emotionally charged situations, our frontal lobe decision-making ability often shuts down, the arousal hijacks our limbic system, which then results in a fight, flight, or freeze response. We will discuss this more in depth in the third section of our book. It is important to keep in mind that the adrenalin response to fear often cripples our ability respond from a rational, grown-up perspective. We strike out in ways that ultimately injure others and our relationships, not to mention our self-esteem.

In her book, *Facing Codependence*, Pia Mellody points out the "lack of moderate" is one of the most obvious signs of codependency to others. *Moderation is essentially a self-containment issue and is related to both boundary and reality issues.* When an individual contains himself with a wall, he tends to shut down and wall others out. In this process, he loses control of being in control of himself and others.

When an individual has no boundaries with which to contain himself he will do whatever he wants to do, disregarding his impact on others. In this process, he might try to control by being out of control and others will have difficulty being rational.

When we are anxiously attached, our inability to trust the intentions and behaviors of others will often lead us to escalate situations and then reject attempts to reassure us. It is a painful and dramatic spiral.

Whether Allison comforts Lisa or becomes even more secretive, she will have resentment she is unable to voice, may well feel controlled by Lisa's outburst, and even bullied into reconnecting with her. Lisa doesn't trust that Allison would miss their connection, or realize that something else, like addiction, might be happening.; she doesn't trust that Allison would seek her out unless Lisa makes some form of dramatic statement designed to "make her aware" of Lisa's presence.

There is a developmental task in infancy called "object constancy" which allows a child to learn that he/she remains connected to their caretakers even when the caretaker is not physically in their presence. It is a hallmark of secure attachment. Anxiously attached codependents frequently have incomplete maturity in this developmental task, and we truly don't trust the attachment when we perceive there to be a physical or emotional absence. We believe, "out of sight – out of mind." This means strong statements of our presence are needed, which could include stalking behaviors, tantruming, throwing scenes, obsessive calling, hacking into other's e-mail, etc. A moderate response never quite seems enough.

Eileen moved home 2 years ago with her two children for the second time after leaving her husband due to domestic violence. Leo and Martha had sheltered Eileen between multiple bad marriages over the last 20 years, and with each separation Eileen's drinking appeared to get worse. Martha had lost her father to alcoholism when she was 21 years old and remembers his death as agonizing and painful. She is terrified at the thought of reliving this experience again with her daughter, and has paid for rehab after rehab in an effort to keep this from happening. She sees the fear in her granddaughters' eyes when their mother is drunk, and remembers her own fear when her father was drunk and out of control.

Eileen had completed another residential program successfully two years ago when she moved home and things had begun to stabilize. Martha and Leo began to hope that they would have a "normal" family and that Eileen had finally "grown up." Martha began to suspect that Eileen had returned to drinking and hiding the evidence, such as bottles. She had become less forthcoming about her activities during the day, and since Eileen was working from working from home while Martha and Leo were running their small print shop, Martha had no way to monitor her activities. Martha began to find opportunities to scroll through Eileen's phone, read old texts, and recently had begun to search through her brief case when she was out of the room.

One night, committed to "catching her in the act," Martha left the house in her car, and drove down to the end of her own court and parked with the lights off. She sat patiently, and after a while saw the cab light in Eileen's truck come on, but she did not get into the car. Martha kept her lights off, sped into her own driveway, threw open the garage door, and caught Eileen with a bottle. "I knew it!" she said. Eileen just stared at her, and took a drink from the bottle. "Congratulations," she said. Of the two of them, in that moment Martha was clearly the most out of control and appeared frenzied. Her therapist later asked her, "When you were stalking your own house, what did you think you were going to do if you caught her?" Martha had not planned on the next step – she just wanted to be right – to prove she wasn't crazy – and wanted Eileen to take her pain seriously.

Martha's frenzied protest was not just a response to Eileen's return to alcoholism, but her fear of the return of an abandonment cycle by her own father in her own childhood. It is common for codependents to not trust their perceptions of reality, and seek reassurance and confirmation that what they are experiencing is real. This is especially challenging when living with an active addict or alcoholic who is compelled by their own denial to minimize and hide the reality and severity of their substance use. It truly can feel like a "cat-and-mouse" game, with a very painful ending.

Martha grew increasingly out of control as she attempted to "manage" what was truly an unmanageable situation over which she was powerless. When anxious, codependents' will frequently throw energy at a situation, in a frantic attempt to use the "throw it all against the wall and see what sticks" approach to problem solving.

Symptom Five: Denial of Dependency or Attachment Needs

John Bowlby pointed out the developmental importance of being able to return to our attachment figure for comfort in the face of perceived threat or discomfort. For avoidant/dismissive codependents, the caregiver was most likely not able or willing to consistently comfort, and may have even been punishing when comfort was requested.

We may have been ridiculed or shamed for requiring reassurance or for having negative emotions about the caregiver. It is possible our caregivers could not tolerate any negative emotions about them or directed towards them, and may have even threatened abandonment – "You could always just go live somewhere else," or "So get a new mommy if you don't like the one you have!"

Some of us may have simply been ignored when expressing our needs, and we became fiercely self-reliant to avoid the pain of neglect or non-responsiveness. Ultimately we become our own secure base, distrusting the capacity of others to provide our needs. We become counter dependent – if I can't provide the need for myself, then I will do without. We will not risk possible rejection or non-response when asking for help. If we are forced into accepting assistance, we will feel obligated to return to help ten-fold. We assume assistance always comes with strings attached, and we are unwilling to be placed in such a vulnerable position. It is unacceptable to "need" others in any tangible, structural way.

Larry's son Tom was a talented musician, a graduate of the Julliard Institute, when he was asked to play with a local band. Larry was somewhat disappointed that his son would choose to use his obvious talent this way instead of joining a prestigious symphony that Larry has expected Tom would choose.

Though skeptical, Larry initially found that he enjoyed attending their performances and was proud of Tom. As the band became more successful, Larry started to notice obvious changes in his son – an irresponsibility that had never been present before. His son would at times say hurtful things, and then claim to only be joking. He noticed that Tom seemed to never answer his phone before 3:00 in the afternoon, and when he would ask Tom about it, Tom would be hostile and defensive and tell Larry to "get a life."

Despite his concern, Larry didn't want to irritate Tom, and figured Tom was probably right -he was being intrusive and he should let the boy alone. Larry felt he was being a "good father" as he increasingly found new interests in his life, spent more time on his hobbies, and began

to operate with less and less expectation of his son. He simply withdrew more and more of her energy from Tom, giving him the "space" he seemed to want. It never occurred to Larry that Tom might miss his company, or that he might be hurt that Larry didn't seem to notice or mind his absence. In fact, Larry was shocked when he was invited by the Family Counselor at a local rehabilitation center to attend "family day." He had no idea his son was an addict, and was especially surprised to find out his son had felt abandoned by him. Larry was just trying to be a good Dad and not "bother" Tom.

Avoidant/dismissive codependents learned early in life that their presence is experienced by the parent as intrusive or demanding, and they quickly adapt with self-sufficiency so as not be such a "bother." Of course Larry would assume that the best thing he could do to be supportive is to "get out of the way" rather than distract Tom from his goals with his needs and wants. It must have been so confusing to see his attempts to please Tom (by disappearing) so unappreciated, and then to be "rewarded" with betrayal! Because he feels so disposable it is relatively easy for him to react with an "out-of-sight, out-of-mind" behavior.

Avoidant/dismissive codependents are often oblivious to the detached messages they give to others, even those they would describe as "intimate" others. While we very much want to be needed (shoring up others' attachment to us), we are constantly on guard to keep anyone, including ourselves, from witnessing any "neediness" or "dependence" we may have in a relationship.

We allow ourselves to love and be loved, but not enough to entrust our security to another or share our position as our own "secure base." Childhood experience taught us that this was not wise and we may feel lonely at times, but are unwilling to trade full participation at every level in order to reduce this loneliness.

Symptom Six: Avoiding Intimacy

When others attempt to penetrate our self-reliance we can exhibit a variety of self-protective mechanisms designed to "appear" intimate without actually being intimate. We participate in the "counterfeit emotional involvement" discussed in the developmental section. With intimacy comes the possibility of "engulfment," being taken hostage by the demands of others. We may have distorted perceptions of the "demands" and obligations placed upon us by those who claim to love us. Trusting love to be unconditional is almost impossible for us and we are always scanning for the unstated subtext or hidden agenda connected to this love

Our fear is that we will allow ourselves to become "dependent" on someone for structure and support, only to experience the abandonment or non-response our "internal working models" tell us is inevitable. We invest a certain amount of "pride" in our ability to maintain our "self-sufficiency." This pride may prevent us from allowing others to give to us. We reject their offers of presents or dinner invitations to avoid the "tab" we expect to pay at a later time.

Terri was visiting her grandmother after her discharge from 60 days in a residential center. As much as she enjoyed her grandmother's company, she wondered why her grandmother had very few phone calls. Even though she was in her late 70's, it would irritate Terri's grandmother if Terri offered to assist her in some way. Her grandmother interpreted offers of assistance as a statement that she was pitiful and worthless. Terri was already struggling with believing in her own competence and it would have been very helpful for her to be of service. Unfortunately, she interpreted her grandmother's "rebuffs" as a statement that her grandmother felt she was too stupid to be of use.

Her grandmother enjoyed playing bridge, and one afternoon one of her bridge friends called and invited Terri and her grandmother for brunch on Sunday. Terri watched as her grandmother hung up the phone and began to be agitated and uneasy. When Terri asked her about this, her grandmother stated, "They just want us to come over to see their new house so they can show off. If we accept, then I'll be obligated to have them over, and my apartment isn't set up to entertain. I don't know what they really want." Terri was startled by her grandmother's perspective, and suggested that it was possible

that they simply wanted to have them to brunch because they liked her! This caused her grandmother to "snort" in response, wagging her head at Terri's naiveté. It then occurred to Terri that her grandmother may not have invited her to spend time with her after rehab not simply because she loved her, but because she felt obligated and was in fact, burdened by her presence. The more Terri pondered this possibility, the more she felt like drinking. Terri's grandmother would have been shocked at this perception because she did, in fact, adore her granddaughter, but had no effective way of accepting Terri's attempts to show attachment and affection.

As her grandmother, it is quite possible that Terri's parents shared this same distrust and disdain for attempts to help and share responsibility. It is possible that Terri has never been able to participate in her family structure as a competent, giving person due to everyone's excessive self-sufficiency. Attempts to bond may be interpreted as "needy" which would be met with strong disapproval.

This leads me to think about Codependents who crave attachment at one level and avoid intimacy at another. Even when we do connect with others it can feel somewhat unsatisfying due to our lack of attunement, like one cookie. It is strange how we can appear so engaged, yet the Plexiglas between us and the other person remains carefully intact. The vulnerability of being completely emotionally honest and exposed can be excruciatingly anxiety provoking. It creates anxiety for us when we are exposed and when people around us are in pain. It is so much more comfortable to be DOING something (anything) rather than remaining in an exposed feeling state.

Lack of willingness to be vulnerable also prevents us from allowing others to take care or support us. We anticipate the needs of others (earning our value) yet frequently leave others no way to express their love to us by taking care of us. A man who loved me once told me, "You don't NEED me for anything." And he was right! I never wanted to give anyone that much power over me. My paranoia, (the typical paranoia of a particularly avoidant codependent) looms large when strong emotion comes into play or when others express a desire to get closer to me. What if they find out I am needy? What if I find out I am needy?

Some of us were raised with caregivers who found our presence intrusive – consuming valuable resources they needed just to cope with themselves or the chaos in their adult relationships. Asking for what we need or want caused them anger or distress, and we quickly learned that the best way to be supportive is to handle our own business and not be a "burden" to those we love. If they did provide what we needed there was always a cost incurred – a tab was due later. Usually, this "tab" included submitting to controlling requirements, demands, or guilt. For this reason, we often chose to simply not have what we needed rather than suffer the guilt or control. As adults, we look for the tab or unspoken agenda even when there is no other agenda. This is why we can appear so suspicious or rejecting of offers with support or assistance.

Symptom Seven: Walls Instead of Boundaries

If our compensating style is one of compulsive anticipation of other's needs, we can appear to be more accessible than we actually are. We are often highly available to others, careful to not "burden" others with our issues. We avoid allowing ourselves to express any need for comfort. After all, people may fail us or be unresponsive. We may even have "Teflon coating," where the disappointments and heartaches of life seem insignificant to us as we persevere in the face of challenges. *It never occurs to us to ask for assistance.*

If we need to have the couch moved we will find a way to move it ourselves. If we are ill we go out to get our own medication and chicken soup, then hole up in our home until we are "fit" to return to the world with our image intact.

Anne Wilson Schaef refers to this as *"impression management,"* where we spend a great deal of energy managing other people's feelings and impressions of us. If we are honest with ourselves, very few people actually "know us" at an intimate level (though they may have the impression they are closer to us than they are). In fact, people who love us would be surprised by how little we trust them or expect them to be available, and how vigilant we are for signs of the impending disloyalty or abandonment. We always have an exit plan ready for the "inevitable" broken attachment. This justifies withholding parts of ourselves and sets the stage for our self-fulfilling abandonment process.

If we have a grandiose streak, we may even begin to believe our own image and see ourselves as super-competent. We may even judge others (albeit silently) for their weakness of getting dependent on others and then "broken" when the relationship is disrupted.

Have you ever judged someone else as "weak" who admitted to needing someone else?

Ruiz and Maria had immigrated to the US in the 1950's, and their story embodies the "American Dream." While they were not educated themselves, they worked multiple jobs to educate their children to provide them every opportunity they could to help their children to fully assimilate into the new country. It was understood that the children's' only obligation was to become successful in life, which also honored their parents' sacrifice in the new country. As each child completed high school, and then college, Ruiz and Maria swelled with pride, tearful with gratitude for the health and success of their children.

Ramon was the youngest of the children, born 5 years after the last child, and was often indulged by his older siblings as the last "special" child. Maria was reluctant to set limits with Ramon, knowing that once he left her life would change dramatically. Much to the irritation of the rest of the family, Ramon was given more latitude with his behavior. When he would break curfew, he was excused, with the rationale being "boys will be boys." When he would come home drunk and be disrespectful, there was the excuse of "it's just a phase." Ramon managed to finish high school despite his frequent tardiness, and Maria and Ruiz became distressed that he could not seem to hold a job. Relatives would find employment for him, but he would not show up, or leave without explanation. This was very embarrassing to Ruiz and Maria, as their other children had done so well.

Ruiz had abused alcohol when he was growing up, as did many of his cousins and Uncles. However, when he came to the United States he made a decision to "grow up" and make his family his priority. So, he stopped drinking. He did not recognize his difficulty with rage and irritability may be connected to his former drinking – he just felt that he was a passionate person.

When Ramon called from the police station, arrested for a felony DUI after injuring someone in an accident, Ruiz called on friends and family and came up with the bail money, terrified to leave his son in such a bad place. The attorney recommended that Ramon enter alcohol and drug treatment to reduce his charges, and Ruiz and Maria were asked to spend $10,000 on a local program. They took out a loan on their home to make this happen.

It quickly became obvious to the family counselor that Ruiz was extremely skeptical about the usefulness of treatment, and he had even less regard for the Twelve Step program. He felt that he had simply made a decision to "grow up," and it was time Ramon did the same. Ruiz blamed Ramon's behavior on pampering from his mother, and felt the real solution was for Ramon to be a man. Ruiz politely declined offers for family counseling, stating that his family was good expect for Ramon, and objected to the idea that Ramon would attend 12 Step meetings in Aftercare – "he should be finding work and handle his business." Ruiz is very clear that if Ramon does not fix his problem and stop shaming the family, he will no longer be accepted into the family. Maria has seen Ruiz take this position with other relatives, so she knows he is capable of following through on this threat and she is frightened.

Avoidant/dismissive codependents are able to detach from relationships with relative ease. Due to damaged "object constancy," we are quite capable of "out-of-sight-out-of-mind" reactions when co-workers leave or someone dies, which is why we suspect others feel the same way about us! Even though we truly do love the people we are now separated from, those people were never in a position to radically disrupt our lives with their absence. We comfort ourselves with our intact structure and daily routine. This provides the ability for us to act as our own secure base.

There are so many ways to avoid intimacy, and they are worth reviewing here:

Silence – I will not let you into my internal reality. You are required to "guess" what I am feeling and thinking.

This is the "What's wrong? Nothing" game I grew up with. It usually has a backdrop of slammed pots and pans in the kitchen or brooding silence with no communication. If you persist in asking "What's wrong?" long enough you might get, "Well, you should know."

Many of us were raised with the "guess what's wrong with Mom, Dad, Grandma, Uncle, Brother" game that could consume countless hours of anxiety because as good Codependents we want information so we can devise our next strategy. It's a powerful game on the withholding end as silence can be deafening, and if you get really good at this you can ignore everyone around you for weeks. It's a manipulation usually defended by "It's better than saying what I am really thinking or something I'll regret later." However, silence is a communication. Ignoring other people or dismissing them as though they don't exist is just as loud a "Screw You" as drawing it on the wall in crayon. Everyone gets the point when being "punished" in this way.

Anger – A wall of anger creates an invisible ring of distance between us and the world around us. People will go out of their way to avoid angry people, even change paths as they walk to avoid the person who "radiates" anger. Codependents can weigh in on either side of this one. We punish others (who obviously deserve it) with rage when they have it coming, yet we are completely cowed at the mere thought that someone doesn't like us or is mad at us. Other people's anger creates enormous anxiety for us by signaling a potential broken attachment. Uh Oh! We will move heaven and earth to manage their anger. It doesn't scare us when we are angry because we KNOW we aren't leaving but we aren't so sure about them.

And aren't there so many ways to demonstrate anger? Some of us are masters at the dismissive disdainful tones, implying we are addressing a moron or someone of low character. Some of us are quick witted and sarcastic – quick to find amusement in the misfortunes of others or small peculiarities about them. Some of us are far more comfortable taking the judgmental/critical path of anger, outlining the mistakes and failures of others in clear detail. Then there are those of us who believe it is our mission in life to "teach" others. We frustrate or confuse them in order to make them "learn" a lesson we feel qualified to teach.

Compartmentalizing – We carefully keep some parts of our life separated from others. We have groups of friends that don't know each other, or anything about our other interests. It's normal to share different aspects of ourselves with others who share similar hobbies or interests. Sometimes we have our work friends, our recovery friends, our friends from high school, our gym club friends, etc. The problem comes in when these aspects of ourselves become secrets that keep parts of us closed off.

For example:

- No one at work knows I am married
- No one in my book club knows my real profession or my name
- My family has never met my drug using friends and doesn't even know they exist.

I begin to have separate lives, whole other personalities and conversations that never over-lap. My partner may know nothing about where I work or what I do. This lack of disclosure and transparency helps us to never be fully available or present in ANY relationship because no one knows all of us. Intimacy becomes impossible at this point.

The internet particularly fosters this trait if you are predisposed to it. You can create entire websites or identities where you can lose yourself in fantasy. Over time some people forget how to come back to "reality," preferring the imagined self to the reality of who they are.

Depression – Depression causes us to lose our ability to focus, concentrate, retain information or have the energy to function at our best. It feels like "walking through mud" and we often will appear numb – not sad – so conversation and connection becomes difficult. Depression can lead us to tolerate situations that truly are intolerable, and convince ourselves nothing will change so "why bother?" Symptoms of depression tend to include unfounded guilt and critical self-talk. We ruminate over things we should or should not have said, worry about other people's feelings about us and lose our ability to see hope for the future. We give up on ourselves, and may even give up on life.

Busyness – Some of us take a perverse pride in lamenting about how we are overwhelmed by to-do lists, endless responsibilities and obligations. Our sense of importance is only matched by our sense of victimization because no one works as hard as we do. Of course, the busyness is usually about other people's needs and demands. We over schedule ourselves and run like a chicken without a head from one activity to another. We grimace as we arrive late to yet another appointment we shoved in between other commitments.

We have no idea our busyness communicates to others how we are unavailable and even self-important. We see ourselves as modest in our over scheduling because so much of it is for other people. It is a wall between us and other people, creating guilt for people around us who may need or want our attention. The people we are doing all of this for may in actuality feel lonely around us, wishing we would just stay home tonight or just get a cup of coffee instead of running around trying to prove our value. Our distorted thinking makes us believe all this activity makes others want us. Without all this activity we would be boring or have nothing to offer. The truth is, with all this busyness we have nothing left to offer.

Passive – We don't initiate or respond in a timely a manner and do not state our preferences or desires. It is very hard to know someone who simply "waits" for direction. Passive people also give the appearance of not caring and not being invested. This happens when we are hesitant to declare our needs and wants, fearing to impose or be "bossy." People have no way to please us or surprise us because we never state our preferences or ask for our needs or wants. We see ourselves as easy-going, or going with the flow, but in reality we are like clear jello or a piece of furniture. We have no enthusiasm for life – no expressions of joy or passion that might possibly be in conflict with the needs and wants of those around us. We are so terrified of conflict we are barely alive.

So we wait, hoping for what we want. Or we "hint" at it, because actually asking for what we want is just way too controlling or bitchy. We try not to takes sides or put people off by being too definite or opinionated. We value our ability to see all sides of an argument. We feel this makes us very fair. What it actually makes us is wallpaper.

Indecisive or confused – We are unwilling to commit to direction or plans, always leaving the window open for another possibility. We take ambivalent stands on opportunities and often let life pass us by due to our fear of commitment or being trapped. The avoidant Codependent wants to know all their options, and always makes sure there is an escape clause. Allowing ourselves to get committed could mean we might have to fully show up, be intimate or even open ourselves to accountability and the expectations of others. We get in a situation where our lives are taken over by the inconvenient and smothering demands of others. Someone will swallow us up and take away all our freedom!!!!

Someone wanting to share our life does not automatically mean that they will control the shit out of us and start micromanaging our lives. We can retain our option to continue our independent interests and growth. We can continue to be a separate person. In fact, when someone wants to marry us it doesn't mean they are wanting to enslave us and spend the rest of our lives bossing us and blocking our life choices.

Incompetence – If we consistently perform tasks badly or unpredictably, it becomes impossible to rely on us and people stop having expectations for us. We sit on the sidelines and watch everyone else perform from a safe distance. This is relatively rare for codependents, but we do occasionally hide the full extent of our talents or intelligence to prevent others from feeling threatened or even worse, not liking us. We will sometimes defer action to allow others to step in and feel important, often denying knowing what we know so others can feel good about themselves teaching us something. The one piece of dating advice I remember getting from my Mother was, "Honey, get them to talk about themselves and what they are interested in. Then they will think you are a great conversationalist. They will have a good time and ask you out again."

What happens when we follow this advice? We spend the entire evening monitoring the other person's approval of us. "How am I doing? Do they like me?" We disregard how they sound like a braying jackass, not showing one bit of interest in us the whole evening. In fact, the worst case scenario is Mom's advice works and we are stuck going out with him again!

Related to this is our tendency to ignore our intuition – our gut-level read on a situation. We let our thinking override our common sense. When a man is rude to the waitress at a restaurant, flips people off when driving in ordinary traffic or tells you what an asshole he is... he is telling you the truth! He is not telling you this because he has low self-esteem which your love will heal. I promise.

I remember a guy I was just getting interested in when he told me he had just broken up with someone. Why? Because when he has low self-esteem moments he tells her she could do better and suggests they break up. She went through this 5 times before she stopped taking his calls! My first thought was, "Good you're single." Thankfully, my next thought was, "I hope she stays strong and gets somebody who won't stress her out like that."

Here's another one. Years ago I was completely smitten by a man who finally asked me out. We were walking along the beach as he told me about his insane last partner who was so desperate to find out how he felt about her that she went to see a psychic. He told me that story as though SHE was nuts. What I thought was, "Poor lady. She was so confused about your feelings for her she had to get a psychic to try and figure it out. She couldn't get a straight answer from you." Needless to say, I never knew either. Someone else told me he got married and moved away.

Hysterical over-reacting – Over-reacting trains others to dread the consequences of giving us information or telling us how they really feel. People begin to shield us from parts of their life to avoid having to expend energy calming us down. If they tell us they're upset they will have to stop being upset in order to deal with our "upset" over they're upset! It's just not worth it.

This game is related to the "What's wrong?" game. Only it's the "Don't tell" game. We absolutely don't want to deal with the barrage of words and anger and anxiety we will face if we risk telling the hysterical person our honest reactions to the world around us. We shield them (and ourselves) creating a wider and wider intimacy gap. When a woman tells me, "He never calls when he's running late." I always ask, "What happens when he does?" If she's a yeller, I point out that he has to be yelled at twice then, once on the phone and once when he gets home. If I were him I would just wait until I got home and skip the extra inning. If we ask for something we need or want from our partner, like a date night, and they go off on a rant about how they never do enough for us, we're never satisfied... it becomes easier to join a scrapbooking club or travel with girlfriends. At least we won't have to hear about it later. Unless of course, they whine about having to "do everything" while we are out "gallivanting" at our once a month book club.

Over-reactive people show no sense of proportion. Whether it's a serious physical injury or the printer's out of ink, their level of intensity is the same! I learned skills to manage this type of reactivity because my father was like this. God bless him, he would get agitated over just about anything. "Don't drop that." "Better get under it." "How much is that going to cost?" A scratch on the car or shutting the hatchback too firmly would be a DISASTER! Obviously, this breeds a desire for secrecy and lack of accountability because the consequences (if you admitted something) would be out of proportion to the event. It was way easier to just handle it yourself and not ask for help than listen to it. Doing things that prevent people from becoming anxious (and escalating) became second nature to me. Part of my recovery is to be able to tolerate other's anxiety and discomfort and just let it alone.

Connected to this is all-or-nothing statements such as "you always" or "you never." A sentence that starts this way invites defensiveness, it's inevitable. Listen to your language. Do you tend to use words like "disaster" "horrendous" "horrifying" and other exaggerated terms that ramp up the urgency of your statements? Other people might be disappointed but you are "devastated." Other people might be anxious but you are "terrified." The down side of this communication style is forcing people around you to downplay your concerns and not take you seriously. There is no way to determine if something truly is an emergency or crisis.

I had a co-worker who would sometimes list 3 or 4 things he would have to do during the day, all of which could be done in a couple of hours. He'd declare, "I am overwhelmed, there is NO WAY I can manage this workload today." Of course, he could and did. He was perfectly capable. However, he would spin himself up to this level of distress by 9:30 am! At first I would offer to help. Eventually I just stopped listening and wasn't as responsive when he really DID need my help because I couldn't tell the difference. It was the only way I could survive the constant onslaught of anxiety. I saw my mother do the same thing with my father over the years to manage him. She called it "tuning him out," and needless to say it didn't contribute to a very respectful foundation between them.

Blaming and Criticizing – This is a powerful distancer. We identify who is to blame for every situation but then make sure to tell the person (in detail) about their error or mistake. Some of us are quick to manage our shame over any possible error we might have made by pointing to ways we were caused to make the error in the first place. Identifying who is to blame seems more important than identifying the solution. This is a close cousin to overreaction, because overreaction usually includes blame for whoever is "causing" the overreaction in the first place. This is a shame-based behavior and can be incredibly intimidating. People begin to defer to you to avoid being blamed if they "guess wrong" and so increasingly refuse to take responsibility or make decisions if you will be involved. This leads to the obvious conclusion that everyone else is a moron and if it weren't for you NOTHING would ever get accomplished. And the cycle continues.

This is such a lonely position, as it discourages any true partnership. Partnership requires sharing control and this means TRUST. This is so fundamentally difficult for some of us, and we don't even realize how critical we are. We may actually believe we are "helping" people by pointing out better ways to do things, ways they could be more efficient or save time. We may know we are intimidating at times but believe that if they were competent or "had their shit together" in the first place they wouldn't be intimidated.

Being Judgmental – Pointing out ways others "should" or "must" live their lives keeps our focus completely external. We are so busy monitoring the behavior of others (and hiding our own imperfections) it's impossible to feel safe getting close to us or sharing human frailty. As perfectionists, we truly believe we are in the best position to judge. We may even say things like, "I trust my decisions because I know I have looked at all sides of the problem, so am sure I have made the right decision." The implication of our lack of trust is that others haven't been as thorough. They have likely missed some important factor or data that we have not.

Therefore, as the arbiter of "best" in most situations, we feel justified in pointing out the right way to do things. Our conclusions are based on our exceptional ability to see all angles of a problem and we assume our decision making process is completely objective.

The sad part is we believe our perfection is a positive trait, when it is most likely the feature that pushes people away. It is not possible to get close to people without human frailties.

Our humanness bonds us and creates a need for each other. Our dependency as humans is based on our differing thoughts and strengths and talents. Perfection makes us an island. When we are "perfect" no one can contribute to our lives because we have it all together and appear need-less and want-less. It's not a positive trait in the long run. There's a reason "The Church Lady" on Saturday Night Live was probably single, doing the superiority dance all alone.

Being under the influence – Being under the influence guarantees that people will not be able to penetrate our intimacy wall because we are cognitively, emotionally and physically impaired. Any agreements or promises we make are suspect because the substance eventually leaves our body and we may have no memory of the commitment. We are truly not available for intimacy though we might "seem" more emotional. Emotional is not the same as honest, no matter how it may look. Can Codependent people also be the addict? You bet. The inability to tolerate our emotions or the feelings we suffer from make it common to drown this anxiety with alcohol or drugs. It offers relief from the relentless self-criticism and martyrdom we heap on ourselves. We deserve a little break after all we do for others, right? The doctor is writing the prescription and they know best, right?

Sometimes we use food as a sedative, become workaholics to feel empowered, use chaotic relationships to feel stimulated and needed. There are so many ways to leave the reality of who we are. Staying compulsively busy to be too exhausted to feel. Staying angry and violent to avoid feeling our sadness, despair and pain. Using promiscuity to avoid the feeling of loneliness and alienation we feel when we are alone.

Most of us demonstrate both anxious and avoidant aspects of Code-pendency since the developmental origins lie in our fundamental distrust of attachment. It is human to desire attachment regardless of our fear of it. When an avoidant codependent allows significant attach-ment to occur, anxiety and anxious codependent patterns inevitably appear.

Afraid to Let Go

PART THREE

Ultimately, Codependency is a chronic stress disease which can devastate our immune system and lead to systemic and even life-threatening illness.

CHAPTER SIX

CODEPENDENCY AS A CHRONIC STRESS DISORDER

Codependents may encounter other helping professionals, particularly in the medical field, long before being referred for counseling and therapy. Due to the chronic nature of the stress that comes from being vigilant in our relationships, or using our energy to stay unaware of our thoughts, feelings and behaviors, our body begins to develop signs and symptoms to get our attention. The physical consequences of self-neglect will continue to escalate until we finally have to NOTICE that something is out of balance. We head to the chiropractor, the acupuncturist or the chronic pain clinic hoping to stabilize our bodies without addressing the underlying mechanisms that keep our immune systems down and leave us vulnerable.

Attachment Implications in Developing Chronic Stress Disorders

Maunder and Hunter (27) searched the literature on attachment insecurity over the last 35 years and found that attachment insecurity contributes to physical illness. They determined three ways attachment insecurity leads to disease risk: increased susceptibility to stress, increased use of external regulators of affect and altered help-seeking behavior. "The attachment model explains how repeated crucial interactions between infant and caregiver result in lifelong patterns of stress-response, receptivity to social support and vulnerability to illness."

According to a new study published by the American Psychological Association, people who feel insecure about their attachments to others might be at higher risk for cardiovascular problems than those who feel secure in their relationships. "This is the first study to examine adult attachment and a range of specific health conditions," said lead author Lachlan A. McWilliams, Ph.D, of Acadia University (28). He and a colleague examined data on 5,645 adults age 18 to 60 from the National Comorbidity Survey Replication and found that people who felt insecure in relationships or avoided getting close to others might be at a higher risk of developing several chronic diseases. They found ratings of attachment insecurity were positively associated with a wide range of health problems. "Much of the health research regarding attachment has focused on pain conditions, so we were initially surprised that some of our strongest findings involved conditions related to the cardiovascular system," said McWilliams.

Participants rated themselves on three attachment styles: secure, avoidant, and anxious. Secure attachment refers to feeling able to get close to others and being willing to have others depend on you. Avoidant attachment refers to difficulty getting close to others and trusting others. Anxious attachment refers to the tendency to worry about rejection, feel needy and believe others are reluctant to get close to you.

The participants answered a questionnaire about their histories of arthritis, chronic back or neck problems, frequent or severe headaches, other forms of chronic pain, seasonal allergies, stroke and heart attack. They also disclosed whether a doctor had told them they had heart disease, high blood pressure, asthma, chronic lung disease, diabetes or high blood sugar, ulcers, epilepsy, seizures or cancer. They were also questioned regarding their history of psychological disorders.

After adjusting for demographic variables that could account for the health conditions, the authors found that avoidant attachment was positively associated with conditions defined primarily by pain (e.g frequent or severe headaches). Anxious attachment was positively associated with a wider range of health conditions, including some defined primarily by pain and several involving the cardiovascular system (e.g. stroke, heart attack or high blood pressure).

The authors also adjusted for lifetime histories of common psychological disorders and found that people with anxious attachments were at a higher risk of chronic pain, stroke, heart attack, high blood pressure and ulcers. "These findings suggest that insecure attachment may be a risk factor for a wide range of health problems, particularly cardiovascular diseases. Longitudinal research on this topic is needed to determine whether insecure attachment predicts the development of cardiovascular disease and the occurrence of cardiovascular events, such as heart attacks," said McWilliams. "The findings also raise the possibility that interventions aimed at improving attachment security could also have positive health outcomes."

Attachment insecurity contributes to physical illness through increased susceptibility to stress. For example, anxious, preoccupied attachment involves a self-perception of vulnerability, which may lead to a lower threshold for activating attachment behavior. In this model of hypochondriasis and somatization, anxiously attached people preoccupied with attachment loss have developed a sense of personal vulnerability and vigilance so intense that normal perception of physiological operations is perceived as a potential threat (29). This means bodily responses and sensations could be interpreted as a sign of increasing distress or a "problem." Another example is that avoidant attachment involves an attitude of heightened interpersonal distrust, such that situations requiring intimacy or interdependence (including a situation of apparent "social support") may be perceived as threatening.

Attachment insecurity contributes to physical illness through increasing the intensity or duration of the physiological stress response. For example, Sroufe and Waters (30) measured changes in heart rate in children during the Strange Situation. Heart rate acceleration reflects an aversive or defensive response, and heart rate deceleration reflects attention to the stimulus. The study reported that all children show heart-rate increases during separation, which remain elevated until reunion with the parent. At reunion, secure infants exhibit a soothing calm, returning to their baseline heart rate in less than a minute. Both ambivalent and avoidant children exhibit elevations of heart rate much longer into the reunion sequence, experiencing greater stress.

Ambivalent infants request to be put down before their heart rates recovered to the pre-separation level. Then after being put down, with their heart rates still elevated, they reach up to be held again. Avoidant children show an increased heart rate from the beginning of separation until long into the reunion, *despite the fact that they display very little distress*. These stress response patterns become habitual and eventually account for susceptibility to physical illness.

Attachment insecurity contributes to physical illness through decreased stress buffering through social support. Secure individuals perceive more available support and seek out that support more at times of stress than avoidant or ambivalent (preoccupied) individuals (31, 32, 33). Social support is widely considered to be beneficial to a range of health outcomes (81). Perceiving support as threatening or nonexistent endangers one's health.

Attachment insecurity contributes to physical illness through increased use of external regulators of affect. Since insecure attachment results in deficits in internal affect regulation (34, 35), insecurity is associated with greater use of external regulators. A number of behavioral strategies that are used to regulate dysphoric affect (to soothe, to distract or to excite) are also risk factors for disease, including smoking tobacco, drinking alcohol, using other psychoactive drugs, over-eating, under-eating and engaging in risky sexual activity. For example, adults with avoidant attachment drink alcohol to enhance positive affect (36).

External regulation of negative emotions through food intake has been shown to be a mechanism responsible for obesity (37). Also, attachment style has a strong influence on sexual behavior (38). So any tendency to use substances or external behaviors to reduce stress constitute an increased risk for physical illness.

Finally, attachment insecurity contributes to physical illness through the failure or nonuse of protective factors such as social support, treatment adherence and symptom reporting. In the absence of positive body image, sensitivity to bodily needs or sense of self-control (products of secure attachment) health crises may produce defensiveness and especially denial. Denial of physical condition and needs during a health crisis can defer benefits from supportive resources, increasing risk. Two studies directly support the link between attachment insecurity and symptom reporting. Avoidant attachment individuals tend to report symptoms less often, relying on emotional self-control instead (39). Anxious and preoccupied individuals tend to report an excess of medically unexplained symptoms compared with securely attached individuals with the same disease (40, 41).

Abuse or neglect in childhood contributes to increased risk in adulthood for terminal disease. Felitti et al. (42) found a strong relationship between exposure to abuse or household dysfunction during childhood and several of the leading causes of death in adults. Seven categories of adverse childhood experiences were studied: psychological, physical or sexual abuse; violence against the mother; living with substance abusers, the mentally ill or suicidal or even imprisoned. The health risk factors were: heart disease, cancer, chronic lung disease, skeletal fractures and liver disease. Persons who had experienced four or more categories of childhood exposure, compared to those who had experienced none, *had four-fold to twelve-fold increased health risks for alcoholism, drug abuse, depression, and suicide attempts.*

CHAPTER SEVEN

PHYSIOLOGY OF THE STRESS RESPONSE CONNECTED TO CODEPENDENCY

Understanding the nervous system response to stress is important in explaining the stress-related diseases and conditions created by the chronic stress of codependency. While attachment issues set the emotional and developmental stage for future behaviors, the fight, flight or freeze response is the physical mechanism that leads to our physical deterioration and lowered immune system. The fight, flight or freeze response prepares us to respond to an emergency.

The human body and human mind each have a set of very important and very predictable responses to threat. Threat may come from an external source such as an attacker or an internal source such as fear of abandonment (as is the case with Codependency). One common reaction to danger or threat has been labeled the "fight or flight" re-action. In the initial stages of this reaction, there is a response called the *alarm reaction*

Alarm Reaction

Think about what happens when you feel threatened. Your racing heart, sweaty palms, nausea and sense of impending harm are all symptomatic of this alarm reaction.

During the traumatic event, all aspects of the individual's function-ing change including feeling, thinking and behaving. For instance, someone under direct assault abandons thoughts of the future or abstract plans for survival. At that exact moment, all of the victim's thinking, behaving and feeling is directed by more primitive parts of the brain.

A frightened child in a threatening situation doesn't focus on the words being spoken or yelled; instead, he or she is busy attending to the threat-related signals in their environment.

The fearful child will key in to nonverbal signs of communication, cues such as:

- eye contact
- facial expression
- body posture
- proximity to the threat

The internal state of the child also shifts with the level of perceived threat. With increased threat, a child moves along the arousal continuum from vigilance to terror.

The Arousal Continuum

The arousal continuum is characterized by many physiological changes. Under threat, the sympathetic nervous system increases each of these functions in a gradual fashion:

- heart rate
- blood pressure
- respiration
- glucose stored in muscle is released to prepare the large skeletal muscles of your arms and legs for either a fight or a flight

These changes in the central nervous system cause *hypervigilance.* Under threat, the child tunes out all non-critical information. These actions prepare the child to do battle or run away from the potential threat.

Dissociation (Freeze)

The fight-or-flight response is a well-characterized reaction to danger as we've already discussed. A second common reaction pattern to threat is *dissociation.* Dissociation is the mental mechanism by which one withdraws attention from the outside world and focuses on the inner world.

Because of their small size and limited physical capabilities, young children do not usually have the fight-or-flight option in a threatening situation. When fighting or physically fleeing is not possible, the child may use avoidant and psychological fleeing mechanisms that are categorized as *dissociative.*

Dissociation due to threat and/or trauma may involve:

- a distorted sense of time

- a detached feeling that you are observing something happening to you as if it is unreal — the sense that you may be watching a movie of your life

- in extreme cases, children may withdraw into an elaborate fantasy world where they may assume special powers or strengths

Like the alarm response, this "defeat" or dissociative response happens along a continuum. The intensity of the dissociation varies with the intensity and duration of the traumatic event. Remember, even when we're not threatened we use dissociative mental mechanisms (such as daydreaming) all the time. During a traumatic event all children and most adults use some degree of dissociation, the sense that you are watching yourself, for example. However, some individuals will use dissociation is a primary adaptive response.

For most children and adults the adaptive response to an acute trauma involves a mixture of hyperarousal and dissociation. During the actual trauma, the child feels threatened and the arousal systems will activate. As the threat increases, the child moves along the arousal continuum. At some point along this continuum the dissociative response is activated and a host of protective mental (decreased perception of anxiety and pain) and physiological (decreased heart rate) responses occur. The hyperarousal system begins to slow down.

Today we know the body cannot tell the difference between an emotional emergency and physical danger. When triggered, it will respond to either situation by pumping out stress chemicals designed to facilitate fight or flight. In the case of childhood problems, where the family itself has become the source of significant stress, there may be no opportunity to fight or flee. For many children, the only perceived option is to freeze and shut down their inner responses by numbing or withdrawing into a fantasy world.

When young children get frightened and go into fight, flight or freeze they have no way of interpreting the level of threat or using reason to modulate or understand what is happening.

The brain's limbic system becomes frozen in a fear response. The only way out is for a caring adult to hold, reassure and restore the child to a state of equilibrium which is available if a secure attachment with the caregiver exists. When primary caregivers are not available to soothe and reassure, the child is left to the fight, flight or freeze system without support.

Why is the Fight or Flight Response Important?

Understanding the sympathetic and parasympathetic nervous system response to stress is important in explaining the stress-related diseases and conditions created by the chronic stress of codependency. While attachment issues set the emotional and developmental stage for future behaviors, the fight or flight response is the physical mechanism that leads to our physiological deterioration and lowered immune system. The fight or flight response (named by Cannon and Selye in the 1930s) is a pattern of physiological responses that prepare us to respond to an emergency.

In the animal kingdom the rules of survival are simple: only the stronger survives. When faced with danger, the two main options are fighting (when you perceive the enemy to be weaker or when defending your cubs or herd) and running away (when you encounter a huge hungry lion, for example). In the face of danger the body shifts its inner-balance to high physiological arousal which enables fight or flight. It is designed as a short-term response to threat and the level of arousal is supposed to settle within a short period of time – after the lion is gone.

Let's emphasize two points about this healthy stress response. First, it takes priority over all other metabolic functions. Second, it wasn't designed to last very long.

So, how is fighting a lion related to anxiety about an upcoming meeting with our employer? Our physical response to a perceived threat is EXACTLY the same. When our attachment issues are triggered we physically respond just as though it was a lion. But lions only visit occasionally, whereas we perceive threats to our attachment frequently; up to several times a day. Each time, we experience intense adrenal system arousal and release cortisol (the "rust" of the human body). We'll look at this in greater depth later.

First, we look at how the Autonomic Nervous System (ANS) responds to threat and how that translates into physical damage over time. The ANS is composed of the sympathetic and parasympathetic systems. The ANS affects many bodily functions instantly and directly while hormones have slower yet wider effect on the body. Both hormones and neurons communicate with cells and create the delicate dynamic balance between the body and its surroundings through paired systems and feedback mechanisms.

The ANS is responsible for many functions in the body that occur "automatically" such as digestion, heart rate, blood pressure and body temperature. The activity of the autonomic nervous system takes place beneath our conscious control. It is automatic.

There are two branches of the ANS that are designed to regulate the fight-or-flight response on a constant basis. The *sympathetic nervous system* is the part of the ANS that is responsible for initiating the fight-or-flight response. Each time we have a thought of danger or pain, the sympathetic nervous system initiates the fight-or-flight response to prepare us to handle the potential danger or pain. It is an automatic reaction. *We only need to think that we are in danger* and the flood of physiological and emotional activity is turned on and goes into perfect functioning to increase power, speed and strength. This is key because it means that you don't have to actually threaten to leave me. I can just picture you leaving me and fully stimulate this response.

The other branch of the ANS is called the *parasympathetic nervous system*. This branch of nervous activity is designed to return the physiology to a state of *homeostasis,* or balance, after the threat is no longer perceived to be imminent. Homeostasis is a state of internal stability of our physiology and our emotions. In other words, the function of the parasympathetic nervous system is to slow things down and return us to a calmer state. During parasympathetic activity, blood concentrates in the central organs for such processes as digestion and storage energy reserves. Breathing is slow, as is the heart rate. Blood pressure and body temperature drop. In general, muscle tension decreases. During parasympathetic activity (general relaxation) we are quiet and calm. The body regenerates and restores for future activity.

The autonomic nervous system is controlled by the *hypothalamus,* which is commonly known as the "master gland." The hypothalamus receives the message of danger from the higher-order thinking component of the mind and delivers a message through the nervous system that connects directly to every other system of the body. The hypothalamus also delivers a message to the endocrine system to initiate the secretion of hormones. The hormones, primarily adrenalin (epinephrine) and cortisol, flood the bloodstream and travel throughout the body delivering information to cells and systems which make us speedier and more powerful.

Parasympathetic response systems do not help us operate at high capacity to escape from a lion. Therefore their work is suppressed in order to divert energy to those vital systems involved in increasing speed and power. For example, you don't need the immune system or your reproductive system to help you escape from the lion.

What does the fight or flight response look like in the moment?

In the moment of feeling threatened, immediate and significant changes occur in our bodies, including: increased heart rate, blood pressure and respiration. This pumps more blood around the body supplying more oxygen to the muscles and heart-lung system.

Also, sugar rates in the blood increase, allowing rapid energy use and accelerating metabolism for emergency actions.

Blood thickens to increase oxygen supply (red cells), to enable better defense from infections (white cells) and to stop bleeding quickly (platelets). Senses sharpen. The pupils dilate; hearing is better etc., allowing rapid responses.

The body prioritizes blood flow, increasing blood supply to peripheral muscles and the heart as well as motor and basic-function regions in the brain. Whereas blood flow is decreased to the digestive system and irrelevant brain regions (such as speech areas – making it hard to find our words). This also causes secretion of body wastes, leaving the body lighter.

There occurs heightened secretion of adrenaline and other stress hormones to further increase the response, and to strengthen relevant systems.

Secretion of endorphins also increases. Endorphins are natural pain-killers, providing an instant defense against pain.

There are further systems involved in the fight or flight response and even more consequences to it. It is clear that the fight or flight response is crucial to dealing with some short-term dangers but is incapable of dealing with long-term stress. Any return to homeostasis is always interrupted and access to parasympathetic responses, like our immune system, is suppressed. The grave consequences of long-term stress on our body and mind are a direct result of this suppression, and the over activation of adrenalin systems often leads to adrenal fatigue and chronic illness.

Adrenaline is by far the most important single hormone regarding stress, playing a major role in the stress reaction. The action of the adrenal system is so significant I'm devoting an entire chapter to it.

CHAPTER EIGHT

STRESS AND THE ADRENAL GLANDS

Unlike our ancestors, we live with constant stress. Instead of occasional, acute demands followed by rest, we're constantly overworked, undernourished, exposed to environmental toxins and worrying about others — with no let-up.

Every challenge to the mind and body creates a demand on the adrenal glands. And the list of challenges is endless: lack of sleep, a demanding boss, the threat of losing your job, financial pressures, personality conflicts, yo-yo dieting, relationship turmoil, death or illness of a loved one, skipping meals, reliance on stimulants like caffeine and carbs, digestive problems, over-exercise, illness or infection, unresolved emotional issues from our past or present, and more. The result is adrenal glands that are constantly on high alert.

The Destructive Effect of High Cortisol Levels

What is cortisol? In its normal function, cortisol helps us meet these challenges by converting proteins into energy, releasing glycogen, and counteracting inflammation. For a short time, that's okay. But at sustained high levels, cortisol gradually tears your body down.

Sustained high cortisol levels...

- destroy healthy muscle and bone.
- slow down healing and normal cell regeneration.
- co-opt biochemicals needed to make other vital hormones.
- impair digestion, metabolism and mental function.
- interfere with healthy endocrine function.
- weaken your immune system.

Adrenal fatigue may be a factor in many conditions, including fibro-myalgia, hypothyroidism chronic fatigue syndrome, arthritis and more. It can also be associated with a host of unpleasant signs and symptoms from acne to hair loss.

The Loss of DHEA Production

DHEA (*dehydroepiandrosterone*) is an immediate precursor hormone to estrogen, progesterone, and testosterone. When the adrenals are chronically overworked and straining to maintain high cortisol lev-els they lose the capacity to produce DHEA in sufficient amounts. When DHEA is in short supply, people have a hard time balancing their hormones.

This happens because Mother Nature will always favor survival (our adrenal's primary function) over reproduction (our adrenal's secondary function). That's why hormonal balance becomes increas-ingly problematic as stressed-out women approach midlife. It's bad enough that ovarian sex hormone production declines naturally, when you throw stress on top of that you can see how vulnerable we are to illness.

Over time low DHEA leads to fatigue, bone loss, loss of muscle mass, aching joints, decreased sex drive, and impaired immune function. All these symptoms we look for Hormone Replacement Therapy to replace. Stress masquerading as peri-menopause? It's not "the change" but rather the lack of change we suffer from.

Adrenal Fatigue

Our daughter is now 36. She is a beautiful lady that always had the best in her life. She was a cheer leader and had a circle of friends in her school years that was very impressive. She met the wrong man, and has been on a slippery slide since she was 18. She is now an addict on cocaine, meth… whatever and has been for 12 years.

We have tried everything including counseling for ourselves etc. She even went through rehab, but within a few months she went back to her old ways. Truly, not assisting financially is a must. WE did and she sold everything for pennies on the dollar. She has lost all 3 of her children, and we have them in our custody.

Life is complicated. We ache beyond belief, but we have moved on as best we can. We try and find her on special occasions to make sure she knows who love her and want her back. That is all we can do. She is so frail and so sick, but we have tried everything, including intervention.

So, we wait.

We have another child and we all agree on our stand and we are united and continue to be functional.

Quietly though, I must admit that half of my being is numbed and somewhat dead. It has changed me, the father to a point that I force myself daily to look at the half full glass. *www.dailystrength.org*

Do these symptoms sound familiar? Are you feeling fatigue, insomnia, weight gain and depression? If so, your underlying problem could be adrenal fatigue.

Are your adrenals imbalanced?

Here are some questions to help you check how much strain you may be placing on your adrenal system.

- Are you always on the run?
- Do you feel like you "can never do enough?"
- Does everything seem like it's a whole lot harder for you than it should be?
- Do you find it difficult to get out of bed in the morning?
- Do you use caffeine or sugar to bolster your flagging energy in the afternoon?
- Do you feel weary and irritable much of the time?
- Do you often crave salty foods or binge on sugar?
- Do you fall asleep while reading or while watching movies?

- Do you struggle to "come down" at night so you can get to sleep?

If the answer to more than one of these questions is yes, you may consider talking to a functional medicine practitioner about your adrenal glands.

When a major attachment is broken we feet "bone-weary." It is impossible to concentrate, and we feel as though there is no extra energy to draw upon. The phrase "grief stricken," translates in my experience to feeling paralyzed or frozen at times. The simplest concentration tasks exhausts us. We are irritated easily. We find ourselves snapping at people when they ask things of us. They have no idea how little energy we have to spare. It is a great relief to finally know what is happening to us, that we are experiencing the result of the intense adrenal surges we have been having for years or weeks. Now, we can get into solution for a change and begin moving toward physical healing.

Anyone with these symptoms can get an adrenal fatigue test which assesses cortisol levels. Thousands of people with these symptoms have taken the adrenal fatigue test, and the results: only 10–15% have cortisol levels indicating healthy adrenal function, 85–90% suffer impaired function ranging from significant adrenal stress to complete adrenal exhaustion.

The effects of adrenal dysfunction can be profound: fatigue and weakness, suppression of the immune system, muscle and bone loss, moodiness or depression, hormonal imbalance, skin problems, autoimmune disorders and dozens of other symptoms and health concerns. Be on the lookout! And get tested if you feel you are suffering.

Natural Adrenal Support — How to Restore Healthy Adrenal Function

The first step is a full physical exam. Make certain there are no serious underlying medical issues causing your symptoms. People with mild to moderate adrenal fatigue can see significant improvement through the following simple steps:

- *Enrich your nutrition, reduce carbohydrates, and cut back on stimulants.*

- *Consider nutritional supplements that support adrenal function.* Start with a high-quality multivitamin–mineral complex rich in stress vitamins, minerals, and essential fatty acids. Talk to an herbalist or naturopath to learn how select herbs help restore adrenal balance, and find the best combination of herbs for you.

Adrenal draining	Adrenal restoring
• Drinks that contain caffeine	• Ginseng • Eleuthero/Siberian ginseng (in the morning)
• Alcohol	• Herbal teas like chamomile, passionflower, valerian
• Gatorade	• Vegetable juice (with salt), like V-8

- *Reduce stress, include moderate exercise and take more time for yourself.* It's helpful to make a list of your stressors, especially those that are ongoing or self-imposed.

- *Get more rest.* Your body needs time to heal!

People with more entrenched symptoms or those who have reached complete adrenal exhaustion may need further intervention. Finally, we can never underestimate the power of perceived stress. Guilt, pain from past hurts, self-destructive habits and unresolved relationship problems may be functioning as ever-present stressors in your life. Dealing directly with these problems is far more beneficial than spending a lifetime compensating for the stress they create.

In all but the most extreme cases, you can expect to see dramatic improvement in four to six months. For mild to moderate adrenal fatigue, the turnaround can be faster. Know this: you may feel you're just too tired to make changes now. But by moving forward in incremental stages you'll build the strength you need to stay with it and you will love how you feel when you do!

Afraid to Let Go

PART FOUR

Recovery is Possible

CHAPTER NINE

SPECIFIC THOUGHTS FOR TREATMENT

Symptom one: Lack of Attunement with Self

Our lack of internal and external boundaries, which results in "shape shifting" in response to the needs of those around us can leave us out-of-touch with our own needs and wants.

Addressing this fundamental lack of "self" will require us to tolerate periods of discomfort as we create time where we are left alone with ourselves. Rather than be distracted by projects, we need to spend time in "free play." We may...

- journal.
- create collages with magazines.
- take field trips to galleries or art and wine festivals where we are stimulated without a "goal" in mind.
- experiment at a mall, where we window shop to get ideas to create a living environment that supports our tastes and preferences.
- take small risks and speak with people we normally would not, just to pay attention to our own reactions and responses. Are we engaged, or do we find our mind wandering?
- listen to talk radio shows and practice forming our own opinions on the topics being discussed.
- go to a bookstore and walk through aisles we would normally skip or avoid just to see what might catch our eye.
- try new radio stations to listen to new styles of music.
- attend a cultural festival for a group you know little about, but have been curious about.

If we are the type of anxious codependent who loses ourselves, we will sometimes feel most sane when we are single. In its own all-or-nothing way, it is our experience that as soon as we begin to form a deeper bond, or merge, we will see our own hobbies, interests and focus in life begin to disappear from our calendar. We keep everything "open" in case we are needed. It will feel almost disloyal to hold onto our own lives if it in anyway may contradict or inconvenience those we love. Unfortunately, we also lose touch of our sadness and anger about giving away ourselves, so it erupts at inconvenient times, or in passive aggressive resentment behaviors. Our focus is so completely external, we no longer focus on our internal measurement of self. Those we love are given all the power to define our value and worth, and we spend so much energy monitoring our successes or failures in being what we assume others want us to be.

Developing a "self" means that we can better identify what is NOT the "self." It means that I develop an internal observer that can notice you walking towards me, and notice that my thoughts, feelings, and behaviors are different from yours. With internal boundaries, I can retain my feelings and thoughts even when yours are different, and find this curious or interesting rather than threatening.

If I can see your behavior and feelings as "information" rather than cues to my next "move," then I don't feel responsible for your thoughts and behavior. With internal boundaries I am aware that you have an entire internal life that has NOTHING to do with me, and does not require my intervention or advice or assistance. With internal boundaries I am in control of how much information I share about me, based on our level of intimacy and trust. I recognize that trust takes time. I cannot have "instant intimacy" and still be selective and self-protective. I will share with safe people and withhold from unsafe people, and internal boundaries allow me to see who is who!

Marion and her adult son, Jeff, were meeting with the family counselor at the treatment center for Aftercare planning. Marion had been attending Al-Anon and working with a sponsor for the last month, and

had attended several individual sessions with the family counselor. Marion's primary pattern was conflict-avoidance, and difficulty setting internal and external boundaries with her son who was often verbally aggressive with her, and prone to blaming her when she attempted to hold him accountable for his agreements. As they were discussing the possibility of Jeff transferring to a local Sober Living Home after treatment, Jeff began to get agitated, aggravated that Marion did not want him to come home and live with her after treatment. At one point Jeff began to raise his voice, demanding that Marion tell the counselor the "real reason" she wanted to "get rid of him." Jeff was referring to Marion's desire to move forward in a long term relationship with a man who had witnessed Jeff's verbal abuse several times, and had made it clear he would not be able to live in this situation. "You're choosing that control freak over me!" he screamed, and Marion could feel the tears well up in her eyes.

However, she had prepared herself for this in an earlier session, so was able to say, "Jeff, I want you to live in a SLE instead of coming home because I want to see you begin to live more like an adult. Most of all, I want to have a different relationship with you. I honestly believe this is our best shot to make that happen." Marion still cried while saying it, but did not allow her focus to be shifted, or let go of her position to avoid Jeff's possible feelings of rejection. And strangely enough, the meeting continued without the explosion she most feared.

External boundaries allow me to be aware that I am in control of my physical self, and that I have control over the space around me. I am in control of my possessions and I have choices about how close I get to you physically. I can choose based on my comfort zone and our level of intimacy how much time I am willing to spend with you, and whether or not I want to participate in shared activities.

Boundaries (a separate sense of "self") allow me to use my judgment to take calculated risks about how much I want to invest in relationships and activities. They will tell me when someone is pushing me somewhere I do not want to go. Boundaries allow me to disengage rather than to keep on trying to make dysfunctional situations "work." I have internal permission to make decisions based on my welfare, and not just what is "best" or most comfortable for the people around me.

David and Jennifer were feeling hopeful as they watched their adult daughter, Crystal, emotionally level out and gain clarity in her thoughts. The Twelve Step meetings she had been attending for the last three months obviously been good for Crystal, and they could feel relief as the daughter they knew began to return to them. Crystal had started attending Narcotics Anonymous as a court requirement, hoping to reduce criminal possession charges to a misdemeanor, and was currently getting around by asking for rides or taking the bus. Crystal had wrecked the last car her parents had given her, and the car before that had been lost in impound due to failure to pay excessive parking tickets. In fact, Crystal had a long history of not keeping agreements and financial irresponsibility.

One afternoon, after a meeting, Crystal stopped by the house to ask her parents to get her a car so she could get a job. David and Jennifer had already taken a loan against their home to pay for residential treatment, and had sacrificed their yearly cruise to make sure that Crystal could continue in Outpatient and live at an SLE to meet her court requirements.

As they listened to her request, both David and Jennifer could feel their heart begin to race, and they looked at each other like deer caught in the headlights. Crystal was animated as she justified this expense to them, and hinted that if they didn't do this she would not be able to work and pay her court fees, and the stress might be "too much" for her. They clearly heard her implied message that if they didn't give her the car, she would relapse and it would be their fault. Jennifer could feel her fear of the "worst case scenario" and started to feel like she HAD to make this happen for her daughter. In fact, she started to feel so panicked she thought she was going to have a heart-attack!

David recognized the look on Jennifer's face, and quickly implemented something he had learned at an Al-Anon meeting. "Your mother and I need time to talk about this, and decide what we can and can't do. We aren't going to answer you now, but we'll let you know tomorrow." Jennifer was overwhelmed with relief as she was reminded that she could STOP and WAIT.

How do we develop boundaries?

Internal boundaries are developed by practicing "noticing" what is happening with your body, noticing your thoughts, noticing your feelings, and noticing your behavior. Some of us may find this so difficult that we will have to keep a running notebook where once an hour we stop and write down:

- What I am feeling Physically
- What I am feeling Emotionally
- What I am Thinking
- What I am Doing

Many of us have years of practice deliberately NOT being attuned to our internal reality because we fear our needs and wants will threaten our primary relationships. Don't be surprised to find self-talk that calls you "self-indulgent," "selfish" or "foolish."

Some of us were raised by caretakers who found differences between us threatening to the relationship and saw fusion as a sign of love. They may have become angry and rejecting as we attempted to differentiate ourselves, seeing our choices as implied criticism of them as parents. It is important to invite people to participate in your life who are capable of seeing you as a separate person, even when you have a different preference. It would be great if they enjoyed the fact you have a different opinion and supported your individuality!

Maybe we tell ourselves "it doesn't matter anyway." It may well have been true that self-awareness would have caused us more misery growing up since we were powerless to change the situation. "Checking out" may have saved our sanity at one point. It is also possible once you start tuning back into yourself you may not like what you see. The difference is that you will be tuning in to yourself from a place of empowerment – you have the ability to change your situation at this point and are not at the mercy of significant attachments in your life for your survival.

As Jennifer and David discussed the car situation for Crystal, Jennifer could feel her struggle with fear that she was being "selfish" to not provide the car to Crystal. Rather than feeling selfish, David found himself resentful, "After all we've done for her," and they made the decision to get outside help because they could see they were too close to the situation to be objective. They both recognized that they were having overwhelming emotions, and were open to exploring where their feelings were coming from, so they called a therapist recommended by Crystal's treatment center. Then they told Crystal that they were going to get advice, and so would NOT have an answer for her until they could meet with the therapist. This was good role modeling for Crystal, because as angry as she was, they implemented actions she had learned in treatment. She had been told "it's okay to ask for help," and it was helpful that her parents were modeling this for her.

Symptom Two: Lack of Attunement with Others

You may notice your behavior is intrusive at times or not considerate of those in your life. If so it is possible you operate in the world as though you are invisible because significant attachment figures did not notice your needs and wants. You learned to address them yourself without checking in with others or working cooperatively. Maybe you had to "take" what you needed regardless of the feelings of others because significant attachment figures did not respond to your needs in a timely manner or did not meet your needs appropriately.

Lack of nurturing when you have been "invisible" shows up in a variety of ways. I have worked with people who would not use the bathroom for 8 hours a day at work to avoid "inconveniencing" co-workers who would have to take their position at the front desk for a short period. I have worked with people who didn't eat all day long because it was a "bother" to feed themselves. As a result we don't remember to ask others if they need to take a break when we are driving on a road trip. Or we don't think to offer a friend a sandwich or a glass of water during a visit. Rather than being self-centered it is self-abandoning though it can appear incredibly thoughtless. We don't notice when we are violating other people's boundaries because we don't have any limits on our own behavior. We are generally oblivious to the fact that we affect other people.

It is also possible that you were expected to accurately "guess" the needs and wants of your caretakers, so you never learned social skills like asking people about their preferences. This is particularly true of those raised with the "silent treatment" response. You were supposed to figure it out yourself or you would be shamed and even threatened. Consequently, you operate largely on assumptions about the needs and wants of those you love and act towards them accordingly. If this was your family pattern you will have to monitor your tendency to expect others to read your mind as well.

You will need to monitor your shame when you notice things about you that may be embarrassing or seem "immature." We have pockets of responses that are "immature" because we didn't have the secure attachment bases from which to experiment with behaviors and try out alternative responses. Instead we mastered a defense or an all-purpose response to situations because we hadn't developed awareness of the full range of available emotions, thoughts and behaviors. It is a "learning" issue not a "character" issue.

As we develop a stronger sense of self and a solid internal observer, we trust our impressions of others more, and can tune into ourselves to pick up the unspoken agendas and feelings of others.

We can practice this by...

- watching movies with the sound muted to rely on language and facial expressions to follow the story line.
- "people watching" at malls, and making up storylines based on the way they carry themselves and their expressions.
- directly asking others how they feel and think about situations, and when we "think" we know, check it out by asking

the other person if we are "reading them" correctly. If we are off-base, we can ask them to share more with us so we can learn better "reading others" skills.

- reading books about body language to become more familiar with physical and posture cues.

- finding someone you admire who has good attunement skills, and asking them to "coach" you.

Over time, as you practice internal observation and see yourself more accurately, you will recognize similar responses in other people, and they will seem less mysterious to you. Your ability to "tune in" to others will improve, and so will your self-esteem.

Jackie and her ex-husband, Ken, had been worried sick about their 26 year old son, Michael, as they saw his life stall and watch him struggle to complete classes that should have been completed 2 years ago. They consulted with outside professionals, and decided to hire an interventionist to work with them to figure out how to approach Michael about getting help for the alcohol and marijuana abuse they felt was caused by Michael's depression. From Ken's perspective, Jackie had been obsessed with Michael his entire life. In fact, once Michael agreed to admission, Jackie was on the phone several times a day with the staff, demanding to know his latest blood pressure reading. . . asking for details of this therapy sessions. . . wanting a copy of the assignments he had been given. . . .challenging staff decisions as "too rigid" for Michael and expressing her fear that the staff structure would make Michael's depression "worse." The staff was at their wits end, and Ken was unwilling to participate once Michael had been admitted. Truthfully, he was embarrassed by his ex-wife's behavior, and his long-term strategy had been to distance himself. This had unfortunately left Michael the sole focus and recipient of her energy and anxiety. Jackie was completely oblivious to her effect on Michael and the staff, and felt she was being a "good parent" and showing appropriate levels of concern.

It was time for discharge planning to begin and it was Jackie's "assumption" that Michael would come and live with her. She started researching programs near her home, and arrived for family group with a discharge plan she felt would be best for Michael without consulting him or the staff. Michael had been working with his counselor on differentiating himself from his mother, and had been giving a lot of thought about his next steps after treatment. Moving home with Jackie was not his plan.

As Jackie made her presentation she waited expectantly for Michael to be pleased with her and assumed they would just "move forward." Much to her surprise, Michael was hesitant, non-committal, and unwilling to consent to her plan. As Jackie started to challenge him, Michael looked his counselor, took a deep breath, and began to share what he was learning about his goals, his plans for the future, and what he would need to stay clean and sober. Jackie was stunned. It was obvious to the counselor that Jackie was interpreting this as a rejection, and Jackie's immediate response was, "So you are saying you have to cut me out of your life to stay sober?!" Instead of capitulating to calm her down, which was his usual response, Michael was able to sit quietly and not become agitated. Tears began to roll down Jackie's face as she asked the counselor, "What am I going to do without him?" admitting for the first time that much of her behavior was based on her own fear of loneliness and abandonment. When Jackie was able to see her part, she was able to move into healing.

It is crucial to be attuned to the impact of your adult child's addiction on their siblings, especially with younger siblings in the home. The amount of time, money and energy you expend to address your child's addiction diverts emotional and financial resources from the rest of the family. You may need to be more closely attuned to the impact of your behavior with your addicted child on everyone else in your life, and create boundaries to be available to others you love and who love you.

Charles became addicted after his father, Tim, and mother, Charlene, divorced, and his dad got involved with a heroin addict. At age 11, he was allowed to get high and drink. Charlene tried to help him at every turn — rehab, counseling, providing a place for him, but she has little contact with him because he is abusive and manipulative and full of rage. Currently, he is facing a year in prison and is homeless, but it is not safe to have him in her house because she still has her youngest son at home, and Charles has threatened her and his step dad. Charlene will always love him even while horrified by his behavior, but has realized that she cannot save him and that she needs to protect herself and her family.

She meets him in a public place for safety and helps him in what she believes are non-enabling ways — paying his co-pay for therapy and meeting him for a meal. Twelve step groups have helped enormously. Letting Go does not mean to stop loving someone; to her it means that she can take care of herself, that she can't control his behavior and understands that her son has his own path. She WILL be there for him if and when he seeks real recovery. Charlene has felt tremendous shame about her son's behavior, but has come to believe that though she has made mistakes, like many others, she is a good and loving parent.

Symptom Three: Distrusting the Attachment of others to the Codependent

This is the heart of anxious and avoidant codependence, and fuels the majority of the defenses we develop based on our "working models" about relationships. Whether we are anxious about potential abandonment, or refuse to connect to avoid the inevitable abandonment, we are often way too defended to notice or trust the stated attachment of others to us. Even when people tell us they love us and are committed to us, we are always factoring in a "Plan B." Because our efforts to shore up attachment are often founded on creating a need for us, we can never trust the attachment of others to connect to us as people.

We suspect it is based on what we "do" for them, which makes failure to respond to the needs of others so dangerous. If I fail to meet your needs in a timely manner, even if it means sacrificing my own, you will simply find someone else who can do so. We always feel so expendable, and healing requires us to take risks to "be" with others without taking steps to earn their affection or attachment. This is so frightening for us – it feels vulnerable and exposed. *After all, if you had a "choice" about attaching to us, you might not make that choice.*

This means we need to find ways to be with others in "free play." We need to experiment with spending time with others in unstructured settings where connection and being in each other's company is the prime focus, and not the activity itself. We can...

- get a cup of coffee with someone, and risk sharing something personal about our thoughts, feelings or behaviors.

- invite someone to go on an errand we have been dreading, and letting the conversation and companionship make the task much easier.

- invite someone to take a drive to the ocean to simply sit and chat by the water.

- play cards or a board game with someone as an excuse to "hang out."

- offer to support someone in a task they are dreading by going along just to keep them company, not take on the task for them.

- do art projects together.

We have challenging self-talk in these areas as well, as we may be prone to filter input from others through a certain amount of paranoia – distrusting their agenda and affection for us. We need to catch ourselves testing people to see what they are "really" thinking. This kind of perspective creates an invisible barrier in relationships – it is almost impossible to be intimate with someone who is waiting for you to fail or waiting to "catch you" in a lie.

In all cases, the lie is, "See, I knew you were full of shit when you said you loved me." While it is painful to prove that they don't love us, it does remove the anxiety of not being sure or waiting for abandonment. When learning about ourselves with a therapist, we need to be honest about our own motives in our behaviors toward others. It requires "rigorous honesty" and willingness to apologize if we set someone up.

Angela's adult son, Jeremy, had been clean and sober for almost a year, and his sponsor was going to give him a sobriety birthday party and he was going to "chair" a meeting that night. Jeremy knew his mother had worried about him for years, and he genuinely felt this celebration was just as much for her as for him. He called her with an invitation to both the party and the meeting, hoping she would be pleased to be included in his recovery. Jeremy was met with silence on the phone. Angela hesitantly agreed to attend, and quietly hung up. Angela later called her therapist to schedule an appointment for the next week to talk about Jeremy's invitation. As the week progressed, Angela became increasingly anxious, had trouble sleeping, and preoccupied. As she told her therapist about the upcoming party and meeting, Angela burst into tears, admitting that she just "knew" that everyone there had been told that Jeremy's drinking was her fault, she had caused it by being a bad mother, and was in dread that something humiliating was going to happen that night. Rather than feeling included, Angela was feeling targeted by the invitation, and was anxious about the nature of Jeremy's "share", sure everyone attending would be blaming her.

Angela's inability to trust the motivations and intentions of her son is not unique. In fact, Angela was always suspicious when she was included or singled out for some reason, always assuming the worst. Jeremy would have been saddened to hear how much his invitation had distressed his mother, honestly hoping that she would have been pleased. After all he had put her through; he felt she deserved to be part of something positive in his life.

We need to remember to check our motives when we find ourselves volunteering to do tasks for others. Are we getting busy in order to distract ourselves from our anxiety about the "truth" of others' attachment to us? Monitoring our thoughts, feelings, physical and behavioral cues can give us insight into our motives. Have the courage and honesty to pay attention and acknowledge them.

Kevin was anxious about his daughter, Kelly, as her upcoming program discharge got closer. He carried a tremendous amount of guilt about the effects of his own addiction on Kelly when she was younger, and even though they had processed Kelly's feelings in family group therapy, Kevin did not trust that Kelly had forgiven him. He still felt he had an obligation to her to make up for her childhood. Kevin didn't feel he "deserved" her forgiveness, and as a result met with Kelly and her counselor to offer to take responsibility for all of Kelly's transportation needs for the next 90 days in Outpatient treatment. This would mean a 2 hour commute, both ways, from work. It would also mean that he would have to work at home at night to make up for the lost time from work.

Kelly and her counselor were surprised at his offer, and as they discussed it the counselor expressed concern about his over-extending of his day and how that might take a toll on him and his own recovery. These consequences never occurred to Kevin, and fortunately he was able to see how this arrangement could untimely result in resentment on his part, and create the same unhealthy situation Kelly remembered from her childhood!

Symptom Four: Escalation to Protect the Attachment

This particular symptom of anxious codependency requires skills for emotional regulation and management. We are up against our almost instinctive hyper-response to perceived threats, which is physiological as **well as** emotional. Our heart begins to race, our thoughts race, we get warm and physically restless. This level of anxiety is hard to tolerate and doing something – anything- can seem preferable to sitting still with this level of arousal. So... we make calls we regret, make asses of ourselves and say things we don't mean, all in an attempt to discharge a painful level of arousal that makes us feel like we are coming out of our skin.

We dial the phone obsessively in an attempt to get a response or drive by their home repeatedly to monitor the cars in the driveway. This leads us to immoderate and extreme behaviors that, in retrospect, seem over-the-top even to us! Yet, at the time, it feels compulsively necessary – I HAVE to DO something!

The lengths to which we go to stay attached are truly hilarious. I remember working with a women's group as one woman described being on the neighbor's roof across from her boyfriend's house, with binoculars, monitoring his front window for the suspected "skank" he was seeing. I said, "So what if she was in there?"

She grinned, "I had my bat in the truck."

I said, "Of course you did! So the plan was to barge in, start swinging, and hope he'll think to himself, 'Oh, Yeah! She's the woman for me!' Because we all know nothing says 'I love you' like a new DV charge."

Of course we were in hysterics by this point, mostly because of the truth of that statement. In our own warped way we honestly believe a threat to our attachment to a loved one REQUIRES some kind of statement, like peeing on their leg to mark our territory. It never occurs to us if they aren't willing to respect our relationship we could simply walk away. One of the things a good Codependent prides herself on is that she's not a quitter, for God's sake.

Half the battle with this pattern is recognizing that no one is "making" us react this way. We are truly in control of our behaviors and have options in how to express our feelings. We have to decide not to abandon ourselves, to remain accountable for what comes out of our mouths as well as our effect on others.

Carl and Joan contacted an Interventionist about their 32 year old daughter, Kathy, after receiving a frantic call the night before. Kathy was calling from a boyfriend's house across the country, and as usual her speech was rambling and she was difficult to follow. It appeared that the police had taken Kathy' daughters, Gina and Susan, into child protective services earlier that day after Kathy had been reported by a neighbor to be passed out on the front steps of the apartment building. Carl found himself becoming increasingly agitated, attempting to break through Kathy's intoxication by starting to scream at her, an old pattern. As Joan heard Carl's voice escalate, she was able to recognize it as fear instead of bullying, based on what they had learned in counseling. Joan stood by him physically, gently touched his arm

to call attention to what was happening, and Carl was able to hand her the phone and disengage from Kathy. As Carl walked away, he could feel a lump in his throat as he allowed himself to feel his fear and sadness, and not the just rage he was used to hiding behind.

One of the best therapies around to manage this reactivity is Dialectical Behavioral Therapy (DBT). There are many books outlining this approach quite well, especially those by Marsha Linehan, Ph.D. Two particular concepts relevant for our discussion here are Mindfulness and Primary/Secondary emotions.

One of the techniques DBT teaches to regulate and tolerate difficult emotions is Mindfulness. It's different than meditation in that you don't "clear" your mind. The goal is to learn to watch your thoughts as they pass through your mind without getting attached or stuck on one particular emotion or thought. The technique is designed to teach you to observe your thoughts without judgment. This leads us to the second concept, Primary/Secondary emotions.

Dr. Linehan has observed that we all have our immediate emotional response to events, such as fear or anger or excitement. However, we immediately "judge" these feelings as good or bad and proceed to have feelings about our first feeling or thought. So, my first feeling might have been sadness, but my immediate next thought is to judge this feeling, "That's a stupid thing to be sad about. Don't be such a cry baby." Then I feel shame about feeling sad.

Dr. Linehan says that the true source of our misery is caused by the secondary emotion that is the result of our judgment about the primary emotion. Her premise is if we could feel the primary emotion without labeling or judging it, that feeling (and our distress) would pass more quickly.

The word "notice" is coming up a great deal, isn't it? This is based on my belief that if you cannot see something, you cannot change it. Accurate attunement to the self is crucial for emotional regulation, because it allows me to see situations as they unfold rather than feeling blind-sided by them.

Closely connected to noticing emotions is noticing your self-talk about your emotions and the world around you. Much of our emotional response is driven by our interpretation of events outside of us. For example, if my husband is running late from work and has not called this is only a FACT. I have choices about how to interpret that FACT.

"He's running late because he is avoiding me." = angry, hurt, anxious about the attachment

"He's running late because I am not important to him. Screw him!" = defensive, avoidant, angry

"He's running later because it is the end of the quarter and he always has more workload at this time." = neutral emotions, compassion, not taking it personally

We choose how to interpret the FACT that he is running late. We also have the choice to check out our theory when he gets home. Instead, we will often match our emotions to our theory and act as if our theory is true. By the time he gets home we are in full emotional reactivity. We may even create a self-fulfilling prophecy as a result of directing so much negativity at him that he doesn't want to come home or stops caring about us! At which point we tell ourselves, "I knew it."

Here's a silly example of this. I rent an office in a wonderful building, and the owner is responsible for cleaning the two bathrooms in the building. Sometimes I will go into the bathroom and notice that the paper towels are overflowing in the trash can. As I look at this, I think to myself. "Dammit, the trash needs to be taken out AGAIN. Why doesn't he notice? He uses the same bathroom. I guess he just doesn't give a damn..." The turning point comes when I am leaving the bathroom and can either:

    a) Solve the problem and take out the trash.
    b) Bring it to his attention.

c) Do what I normally do, which is dismiss it from my thoughts as I head back to my office, until the next time I use the bathroom and the dialogue begins again. Sometimes this happens two or three times a day.

I am reminded of just how conflict-avoidant some of us can be as I "endure" the same aggravation over and over again. I prefer to manage my irritation rather than solve the problem or risk upsetting the building owner. I never trust it will be a simple business exchange, instead I fear it will escalate for some mysterious reason just as conflicts seem to "jump off' as a child. In reality the building owner is a lovely man, pleasant to deal with and responsive. He's just very busy and probably oblivious to the problem. Why can't I trust this?

Loretta had always loved Thanksgiving. In fact, her husband, Ned, used to tease her that they had so many children simply so that Loretta could have a large Thanksgiving meal! Even before the five children were born, Loretta always invited the in-laws and all the "strays from the neighborhood" to join her at her favorite meal. In the last three years this had changed, as the meal would be delayed for hours while Loretta would insist on waiting for her son, Randy, to arrive. Last year, the other siblings raised a mass protest, leaving Loretta in tears, and insisted on going forward without Randy. He did finally arrive as desert was being served, obviously hung-over and still smelling like last night's bottle of wine. His siblings barely acknowledged him, so angry about what he had "put them through" as they helplessly watched their Mom become agitated, anxious, call hospitals "just to be sure", and ruminate waiting for him to arrive. She would even beg Ned to go look for him because he may be "dead in a ditch" somewhere. It was painful to watch.

As Thanksgiving drew near, the other four siblings began to talk about it with dread, and one of them suggested that maybe they should get Loretta some counseling, stating that they were not going to participate this year if she didn't. It was just too hard. The oldest sister, Julie, was nominated to have coffee with Loretta and ask her to get help and coffee was scheduled. When Julie presented the idea of counseling,

Loretta became agitated, "Why is this my problem? Why can't you just be more patient with Randy as he tries to find his way in the world? I suppose you want me to pretend he doesn't exist?" Julie had been prepared for this reaction, so hung in there by not escalating with her mother. As Loretta protested, she began to admit her own helplessness, her own fear of Randy's drinking, and even her own dread about the holiday and the loss of the joy she used to have. Loretta finally agreed to meet with Julie and Julie's counselor to make a holiday plan for this year that would allow the family to move forward without being paralyzed by Randy's arrival.

One of the things we can do to track our automatic negative thoughts is to keep a "thought journal." We write down our negative thoughts as we have them and then write an alternative thought or explanation next to it. Knowing we have a long history of interpreting situations through a distorted or fearful filter, we have to learn to ask ourselves, "Is there another possible explanation?"

The more we draw neutral conclusions and recognize how seldom people's thoughts and behaviors are about us, the more we begin to react accurately (both internally and externally). We will make fewer amends and apologies for "jumping to conclusions" and feel more self-respect and self-control.

The counselor had suggested that Loretta be aware of the thoughts that would race through her mind when Randy was late, and practice writing down alternative thoughts in her "thought journal." As Loretta pictured Thanksgiving, she could feel herself tense up and wrote thoughts such as, "What if he's been in a car accident?" "What if he's mad at me?" "Maybe he forgot because he's working too hard?" "Maybe he is still sleeping from last night because he drank too much." When Loretta wrote the last sentence, she felt something inside of her click because it was the most realistic thought. As she thought more about it, this explanation wasn't so scary and it was probably the truth – it had been true the last three years! So, she decided to make this her thought if he was late, to help her manage her fearfulness and enjoy her favorite day of the year. Ultimately, she wanted to "do something" about Randy's drinking. But for now, she could live with her plan.

Symptom Five: Denial of Dependency or Attachment Needs

Both anxious and avoidant codependents deny their dependency needs to prepare for the eventual broken attachment. Bowlby points out that a characteristic of secure attachment is the ability to run back to our primary attachment figures for reassurance and comfort and receive consistent responses. Because we do not trust our attachments, we try not to ever put ourselves in the position of "needing" a secure-based response from someone else. We are terrified of the feelings that accompany abandonment and have a variety of defenses erected to protect us from that kind of pain.

This doesn't mean codependents don't get attached or love, it simply means we are vigilant for the possibilities (if not inevitability) that the attachment will not be there to support us when we most need it. There may well come a time when our attachment figures will decide that our needs and wants are "too much" and withdraw their willingness to provide a secure base from which to operate. Therefore we need to always hold something back in reserve, much like a secret bank account, "just in case."

It reminds me of the saying, "If you don't hope for anything you won't be disappointed." We know others are "human," which means they will always choose their best interests over ours. We keep our expectations of others fairly low. Ultimately, we believe we are the only ones who will look out for us. We call this being "realistic."

God forbid we allow ourselves to admit any need or dependency on someone.

We will...

- have sex with you.
- take care of you.
- let you move into our house.

We will not:

- tell you how much money we make.
- put your name on the lease.

Frequently we fantasize about how to get rid of you whenever you threaten our comfort zone. The people we love would be really uneasy if they knew how many "Plan B's" we have. Ironically, we have back-up plans because we expect THEM to leave.

Where does this fear of being trapped or needing to take hostages and trap other people come from?

Developmental theorists would say that we are connecting attachment with engulfment. If I love you, you will move into me with a U-Haul and take me over, or if I love you I have to drive my U-Haul into you and lose myself in you. We don't have the tools to remain independent and still connected! We don't know how to share power.

If we are a more avoidant codependent we are hyper-aware of the subtle nuances of other people's growing attachment to us. We interpret their desire to spend more time with us or share our lives as the engine of the U-Haul turning over and we begin to take evasive maneuvers. We do this by accusing them of being controlling, by being unavailable ourselves, by compartmentalizing parts of our lives so that we appear to be more available than we are... all of these are in the service of making sure we don't disappear. But it's not the other person that will take away our freedom and self – we will give it away because on the other side of every avoidant codependent is an anxious codependent. If we let our guard down and let them in, we will flip into the anxious monitoring that makes us begin to look and feel insane. The truth is: No one takes us away – We give ourselves away! The person we most fear is us!

If we are to soften this position and entertain the notion of being "dependent" enough to have expectations for others that could leave us disappointed or hurt, we need to address our emotional regulation skills. If I do not trust my ability to be resilient in the face of distress, I am certainly not going to be willing to allow the possibility.

Dominic had left home at 16 years old and moved in with his older brother Anthony to escape the brutality of his father's alcoholism.

Anthony had been young himself, 20 years old and in college, and Dominic assumed the responsibility of getting himself to school and doing his homework, as well as providing meals and clothes for himself from his job at the car wash. He would relax on the weekends by drinking and hanging out with Anthony as his friends. Dominic felt accepted and safe. As Dominic grew older, his oldest son, also named "Tony" in honor of his brother, was born and Dominic became increasingly absorbed in his career in computer design. Dominic began to drink less as he aged, wanting to be clear and was unwilling to lose control under the influence. However, Tony was now 21, was drinking hard in college, and using cocaine sometimes to keep himself awake to party even more.

One afternoon Dominic received a frantic message from his wife that Tony was in the emergency room in ICU after collapsing from a heart attack, most likely caused by cocaine. As Dominic raced to the hospital, he could feel himself start to leave his body, as though he was watching someone else drive and comfort his wife. When he saw Tony hooked to the machines, he felt numb, and his wife became agitated at Dominic. "What's the matter with you? Don't you have a heart?" Dominic began to wonder the same thing.

Dominic brings to mind a quote from Geneen Roth's text, *"Women, Food, and God"*:

> I used to think that the less I showed up the less it would hurt when I lost everything. When people I loved died. When things fell apart. . . The belief, unconscious as it was, that I couldn't handle, couldn't tolerate, didn't have thick enough skin or a resilient enough heart to withstand what was in front of me without fragmenting.

On the other hand, I need to allow for the possibility of happiness and security because that could also happen (even though I never seriously considered it was possible.) In some way this is the scarier outcome because then we have more to lose. If I remain in a skeptical position, reserving my expectations, then I am safe even if guarded and lonely!

Some of us make the decision to explore a spiritual source as our first attempt to allow "dependence." Others find a spiritual source way too vague and are better off experimenting with a person such as a therapist or a sponsor if they are working a Twelve Step Program.

The idea is to allow ourselves to soften some of our hard edges. It requires us to take the risk of "needing" someone for support and consistent response. To see someone or something outside of ourselves as a possible "secure base." A place we can return if we get hurt or need guidance. This is such a foreign concept for some of us that it takes time to adopt. Our original attachment figure should have provided this, but may not have been available so we are inexperienced with the idea of being "nurtured." We may truly have no idea what nurturing looks like or what it entails. Essentially it means allowing someone else to unconditionally comfort us, take care of us when we are vulnerable, to treat us as though we matter. Once you start to allow this you may find you kind of like it, even if you find it slightly embarrassing.

Dominic was scared by his numbness, knowing that Tony was the center of his world. He realized intellectually that he had feelings, so not knowing what else to do, went to the small Catholic church he had grown up in just to sit in the back pew. He was comforted by the familiar smells and smiled at the old cracked chalice in the front of the church. He had not even attempted to pray for years, but found himself in the quiet, simply saying "Help me, help me. Please don't let him die, I don't know how to live without him." He could feel his heart again, and was reminded that he was a human being who loves.

If you are going to begin with a spiritual "secure base" you could try:

- Going on a "God" hunt. A friend of mine describes this as looking for signs of a power greater than yourself as you go through your daily activities. Notice things that are small miracles, kindnesses, or offer you comfort as they unfold throughout the day.

- Working with a spiritual counselor or a sponsor to define this spiritual power as you understand it. You may need to revise your earlier picture of "God" developed in childhood, which most likely resembles the parents you had. If you had abandoning parents it is highly likely you may have an abandoning "higher power."

- Reading spiritual books by people you see as spiritual and you respect, like Mother Teresa, Deepak Chopra, Thich Nat Hahn, or Marianne Williams.

- Making a "God box." You will write your worries down on a piece of paper and put it in the box. Look inside the box a month later and notice ways in which your worries were resolved, maybe in ways you would never have thought of!

If you are going to begin with allowing a person to provide a "secure base" you could try:

- Choosing a therapist and making a commitment to attend regularly. Be as honest about your emotional reality as you are capable of being. Risk calling him/her in between sessions if you get stuck.

- Working a Twelve Step program like CODA or Al-Anon and allow someone to sponsor you. Meet with them weekly to experience consistent and loving responsiveness to your issues. Allow yourself to be treated as a priority.

- Meeting up with a friend consistently to walk or have a cup of coffee. Practice expecting them to show up every time and consistently be glad to see you. Let yourself count on it.

- Allowing someone else to drive when going places or cook a meal for you when you have had a hard week.

- Calling a friend when you are feeling lonely or anxious and share what is going on with you.

- Joining a church or support group and attending consistently so that the group can get to know you and you can begin to trust that they will consistently welcome you and recognize you. Knowing you will matter to each other, your presence would be missed if you were absent, and you would miss them. Allowing yourself to matter to them without overdoing as a volunteer. Experiment with mattering because you are you.

Georgia was the middle of four daughters raised by a single mother. Her mother's life had been hard, and she had attempted to protect her girls by teaching them wisdom such as, "You best provide for yourself because people come and go." The girls heard these messages and took them to heart, especially Georgia. As she grew up and started having her own children, Georgia repeated her mother's pattern of abandonment by her husband and wasn't surprised when he left. Georgia's oldest son, Carl, seemed unable to keep a job. When he was younger, Georgia thought it was just the immaturity of being a boy. However, as he grew older and the pattern persisted and she began to be afraid he might be using drugs like Carl's father had done. For the first time in her life Georgia felt scared. She was finally up against something her common sense and resourcefulness could not "take care of," and she began to lose sleep. One afternoon her neighbor of over 20 years came by for a cup of tea, and as they were sharing family news, Georgia surprised herself by tearing up – in front of a neighbor no less! Her neighbor, Ginny, was surprised as well but instinctively sat still and listened. Georgia took a deep breath, knowing that Ginny also had an addicted son, and hesitantly began to confide her fears.

As Ginny shared her own experiences, Georgia could feel her heart lighten up with a glimmer of hope. While she found it hard to let Ginny in, Georgia actually slept that night, feeling like she was less alone.

Symptom Six: Avoiding Intimacy

When we talk about mattering, we are entering into the intimacy territory, a tough place for anxious and avoidant codependents. If you have been working on attunement with yourself and emotional regulations skills, you will have an easier time in this area. You will know more about yourself and have more to share at an intimate level. What does intimacy mean?

It means to allow someone to see you as you are, without masks or illusions. It means that I am consistently me regardless of the situation we are in.

What you see is what you get – so I am congruent emotionally, intellectually, and behaviorally. There's no pretense.

This requires us to drop the "impression management" skills we have honed all our life to manage the impression others have of us. It is very possible that we over-identify with our image, and believe our own press! We may have been living this way for so long we have no earthly idea how to be any other way. Convinced of our foundational lack of lovability, it seems way too risky to allow people to get close enough to see our humanity. Many of us have been shamed about human imperfections, having been incorrectly taught that making mistakes is terrible, shameful, and completely unacceptable. We are "supposed" to know things without having to ask or being told. Letting someone see us in our imperfection would guarantee abandonment and broken attachment - right?

We don't die when the worst thing that could happen to us happens.

We don't die when the attachment gets broken. Sometimes we begin to live because, like Rip Van Winkle, we awake to find there is a whole other world out there moving forward while we have been in suspended animation lost in other people's lives. We may have forgotten we exist, but the universe has not lost track of us, and the world is still waiting when we emerge, even though the re-engagement is often not our choice, and we are protesting it.

Maybe we never really made a decision to live in the first place which is why we were avoiding intimacy or losing ourselves in others. We were noncommittal about our own lives, afraid to step into our own lives with full ownership and responsibility. Instead, we hid in defensive self-reliance or anxious absorption in others as a way of establishing personal value.

The Shadow

The famous psychoanalyst Carl Jung introduced the concept of "the shadow" to describe the parts of ourselves that we push away or deny because we believe them to be unacceptable. They are qualities we see in others that we hate, that irritate us, that we judge harshly. We use a great deal of energy to deny to ourselves and others that we posses these qualities, "I'm not a jealous person – I don't have a jealous bone in my body". Or "I'm never angry, I just don't understand angry people", or "I am happiest making others happy. I can't stand selfish people." Somewhere along the way we learned that having these qualities can result in abandonment and broken attachments and we are adamant that these qualities can't be true of us. If we do see them, we feel deeply ashamed, and are very afraid other people will find out they are true of us. Others knowing our "shadow" can make us very anxious.

The more of the shadow qualities that I possess, the more guarded I will be against intimacy. I will keep the door on the closet locked pretty tight. However, Jung said we do this in vain, because these qualities will leak out of our unconscious. Debbie Ford, in her documentary on "The Shadow Effect" uses a beach ball analogy. She says to imagine trying to hold beach balls underwater in a pool. Each ball has a label like jealous, bitchy, petty, stupid. And the more balls we have, the more energy we have to exert to keep them under water. But if we get distracted, and our attention is diverted for a moment from stuffing our beach balls, these qualities will pop out, sometimes in an embarrassing way. Such as referring to our wife as our mother, or calling someone a bitch when we never usually curse, or having an affair when we judge others very harshly who have affairs.

Teresa and John had been married for 32 years, and had a large group of friends in their neighborhood. Teresa had been a stay-at-home Mom, and had formed life-long friendships with the mother's of her children's friends, and John had been an active member of the local Kiwanis club forever. They were often envied by their friend s as the "Rockwell Family," with their handsome successful son and two talented and graceful daughters. Even after all the children had grown and left they still had a strong relationship and enjoyed each other's company.

Lately Teresa's daughter, Nancy, had been less responsive on the phone. She was not a forthcoming with her activities during the week,

and sometimes when Teresa would call to talk about the grandchildren, Nancy's husband Bill, would say irritably, "I have no idea where she is. I can't get her to answer her phone." This was disturbing to Teresa, who had been an active 24 hour mom. Teresa had been the neighborhood "hostess" at the house where all the children from around the neighborhood liked to play. Being a "good mom" was the most important focus of her life when the children were growing up.

Being unable to reach Nancy was creating feelings of judgment and anger for Teresa that surprised her. She began to use a slight "tone" when someone mentioned Nancy, and when she did interact with Nancy found herself more reserved. She also caught herself one afternoon "snooping" in Nancy's medicine cabinet and becoming alarmed at the amount of medication she found, and reading her phone texts while Nancy was out of the room. Shocked at herself, old memories of furtive looks her mother would give when hurrying away from Teresa's father's office, and odd silences between her parents came back to her.

Carl Jung pointed out that the path to healing this was to accept all aspects of ourselves, the "good" and "bad" instead of attempting to compartmentalize and discard aspects of ourselves. These aspects are all part of being human and if we can acknowledge them, we will be more in control of their presence in our lives. For example, if I can acknowledge my capacity for jealousy, it means that instead of using my normal avoidant/dismissive attachment defenses, I will protest when our attachment is being threatened. I will be vulnerable enough to let you know I am threatened and that I need reassurance.

You may want to take some time and try this exercise:

A. List 10 qualities about you that you consider to be negative. Now, next to each write a positive use of that quality. For example:

Stubbornness   This can be helpful because it helps me stay committed to my recovery.

Anger   This can be helpful because it gives me energy to change things that make me unhappy.

B. List 10 qualities about you that you consider positive. Now next
    to each write a negative aspect to that quality. For example:

Patience   This can be a problem if I do not set limits when
                it would be in my best interest to do so.

Generous   This can be a problem because I will give things
                to people that they should earn themselves, so
                thezy appreciate them more.

Once we are more comfortable with the various aspects of ourselves
we will have less to hide from others as well as our self. It will feel
less risky to be intimate because we are able to see ourselves more
realistically and with more balance. We are more likely to tell the
emotional truth, and worry less about being judged. There is a lot of
freedom in this.

**Shocked at her "snooping" behavior, as well as old memories, Teresa
decided to talk to her mother about what was happening. As Teresa
shared her concerns about Nancy and her own intrusive behavior, Teresa's mother got increasingly more still. After an awkward silence, Teresa's Mom finally offered, "I thought I had hidden it better." She went on
to explain that there was s time when she had been concerned about
Teresa's father and his drinking, and she had also wondered if he might
be having an affair. She tried to protect the children from her anxiety,
and had never spoken about it with them. In fact, Teresa's father denied having the affair, but did eventually concede that his drinking was
making him less reliable at home and at work, and that he was lying
sometimes to keep his wife from being aware of how much time he was
spending at the bar so she wouldn't see him drink.**

**As Teresa listened she felt faint stirrings of memories, and suddenly
her snooping made sense. Nancy's lack of availability and accountability was triggering the same fears she may have felt about her own
father's unavailability as well as the anxiety she had picked up around
the house growing up. Her instincts and judgment about Nancy's behavior now made sense to her. She made the decision to have an open
conversation with Nancy about her fears, and hopefully stop the family
cycle of secrecy and addiction.**

Once we are more comfortable with the various aspects of ourselves we will have less to hide from others as well as our self. It will feel less risky to be intimate because we are able to see ourselves more realistically and with more balance. We are more likely to tell the emotional truth, and worry less about being judged. There is a lot of freedom in this.

In his book, *7 Levels of Intimacy* (92), author Matthew Kelly defines intimacy as happening when there is a mutual revealing of our authentic selves. Sometimes this is referred to as "in-to-me-see." His premise is that different kinds of communication create different levels of intimacy, and outlines 7 different levels:

1. **Clichés** - Clichés are simple conversation starters such as, "Hello, how are you?" When these are handled with ease and grace, safety is generated and people are willing to go to the next level. If they feel judged, criticized or ridiculed they will go no further. People start here to see if it is safe to connect.

    a. How are you?

    b. What have you been up to lately?

2. **Facts** - Facts can be personal or non-personal facts about the weather, sports, current events; whatever can be addressed in conversation without too much risk. Except in the case of know-it-alls, this is a great level for people to test whether a person is a safe conversationalist.

    a. Non-personal
        i. What was the score of the game?
        ii. What is the weather forecast?

    b. Personal
        i. What did you do today?
        ii. What have you learned recently?
        iii. What have you been reading lately?

3. **Opinions** - The opinion level is the first level of vulnerability, marked by a person's willingness to risk revealing something

about who they are. This is often the level where conversations break down; where disagreements of opinion reveal inflexibility and intolerance. Conversely, if a person is willing to allow others to disagree without rejecting, ridiculing or punishing, the conversation can continue to the next level.

    a.   What are your preferences concerning…?

    b.   What are your beliefs about…?

    c.   What do you think about…?

4. **Hopes & Dreams -** If we navigate safely through the level of opinions, people will often be willing to reveal what truly inspires them. Sharing hopes and dreams identifies what a person wants to become or how they want to live. Being safe enough to entrust others with your dreams prepares you to connect at an even deeper level.

    a.   If you could live any way you liked, how would you like to live?

    b.   If you could live anywhere in the world, where would you like to live?

    c.   What goals do you have for your life?

5. **Feelings -** When the environment is safe enough to be honest with our feelings, only then are we able to feel truly connected. Inviting someone else into our feelings, however, makes us feel vulnerable, and for most people is a difficult obstacle to overcome, depending on how accepting and validating their past experiences have been while sharing feelings with others.

    a.   When in our life have you felt special to others?

    b.   Who in your life made you feel safe, loved, accepted? How did they do that?

    c.   Who in your life made you feel the most rejected, devalued, abandoned, invisible?

    d.   What are you most passionate about?

6. **Fears - Failures and Weaknesses** - This level is uncomfortable for many of us because in our culture weakness is seen as a fault, and past sharing of one's fears and failures may have been met with ridicule and rejection rather than acceptance and support. Conversely when openness on this level is met with care and nurturing, real healing and growth can occur.

    a. What makes you feel like you don't measure up?
    b. What makes you feel like you are unlovable?
    c. What do you think would make others reject you?

7. **Needs** - Sharing our needs in a way that is vulnerable (not demanding) is a sign of maturity, as is the ability to truly listen to one another. Sometimes our conversations lack meaning because we fail to listen or fail to ask the right questions. We fail to listen because we don't know how to subjugate our own needs in order to meet the needs of others.

    a. What do you need in order to be secure?
    b. What do you need in order to be safe?
    c. What do you need in order to be significant?
    d. What do you need in order to be competent?

Keep in mind that moving through these levels takes time – trust is not instant. There are also various types of relationships; sharing your needs and fears may be inappropriate.

In general relationships exist at various levels:

Acquaintance – The co-worker you know by name only, or the neighbor you wave to in the morning. Cliché level primarily, maybe some facts exchanged.

Companion – This is someone with whom we share a mutual activity or interest, which is the basis of the relationship. So, the activity is primary, and getting together is simply a result of the shared interest. This is my "walking buddy" or "scrapbooking buddy". This relationship might move from cliché to facts to the opinion level.

Friendship – The basis of the relationship at this point is spending time together, and the activity becomes secondary. So, if I want to bowl and you don't, I ask you what you DO want to do, because the goal is to spend time with you. Now we're adding deeper levels, such as the hopes and dreams, feelings and fears level. In truly intimate relationship we will add our needs, because we trust the attachment well enough to know that our needs matter.

Lover – In an exclusive sexual relationship, we add sexuality to friendship and companionship to deepen our connection with the other. There is a level of intimacy that sexuality offers that marks the relationship as separate from other friendships, and our vulnerability is increased as the consequences of rejection are higher. We are completely exposed when naked, and we are declaring a boundary around our sexuality.

Commitment – This creates a boundary around our relationship as a whole, which means there is information, dependency, revealing of a depth of needs and fears that is contained within the safety of this relationship.

It is obvious that we can have any one of these relationships with varying degrees of intimacy. There are married couples who exchange cliché, factual and opinion information only. There are companions who share sex as the mutual activity. There are lovers who do not fully commit. What I have described is the path to deepening relationships so that we can gauge the intimacy expectations at each level. Let's take a look at what interferes with our ability to shift boundaries as trust begins to develop.

Symptom Seven: Walls Instead of Boundaries

We have to learn the difference between walls and boundaries. Pia Mellody points out that boundaries serve two primary functions: *Protecting us from the intrusion of others,* and *Containing our intrusive behaviors.* When we looked at lack of attunement with others, it seemed clear that our obliviousness to our impact on other people could lead us to offend them or invade their internal or external boundaries without knowing it. We could tell them how they "should" feel, because their fear or anger makes US anxious or uncomfortable. We could do their laundry to "help" without asking if they would be okay with us sorting through their personal items. We could allow similar behavior from others because of our lack of attunement with ourselves, so we would not recognize that we are uncomfortable until later, and then we may not connect our anxiety with the earlier boundary invasion. One of the goals of therapy is to feel our feelings in "real time" without this delayed reaction phenomenon. The sooner I recognize what is going on inside of me the sooner I can take care of myself or the situation.

When I do not trust my ability to make good judgments, or trust my ability to accurately be attuned to myself and others, I HAVE to have walls to protect me.

We don't need walls because other people aren't safe. We need them because we can't tell the difference between the good guys and the bad guys, and so keep everyone out just to be sure.

Lack of attunement with other's agendas, needs and feelings can make the world around us seem very confusing. We will often say, "I just don't play politics," or "I just tell it like it is. If you don't want to hear 'the truth' then don't ask me." Because we don't understand others, we will often take a position where we don't even try to connect or be tactful. We give ourselves permission to just barrel though situations, with a "take me or leave me" perspective that gives others very little room to maneuver or compromise with us. It's almost as though we expect others to work hard to get through our walls to prove they really love us. This is a lot to ask of other people.

Ginger prided herself on her "tell it like it is" honesty, and had never worried about whether or not people liked her. If they didn't it was most likely because they couldn't handle "the truth." When her adult daughter Arlene began to cancel their lunches with no notice or was getting arrested for possession, Ginger had no problem telling Arlene off – making sure that Arlene knew she wasn't fooling Ginger.

Ginger used "tough love" by not paying her bail, even called Arlene out on her use of methamphetamine with her new "sleazy" boyfriend, pronouncing that "that shit will kill you." While Ginger was probably afraid, what most people, especially Arlene, saw was her anger. Ginger took solace in the fact that she wasn't in denial like those losers on "Intervention," and she wasn't going to let her "druggie" daughter take her down with her.

The key to healing this aspect of our codependency is to identify the various strategies we use to create intimacy barriers in our relationships with others. The challenge here is to clearly see our behaviors for what they are. We have been using these strategies for so long that we have come to believe that "this is the way I am" and misinterpret them not as behaviors that can be changed, but mistakenly as our character.

Ginger received a call one night from a private residential treatment facility, who had been contacted by Arlene because she wanted to get clean and sober but didn't have the financial resources to pay for the treatment. She asked them to contact her mother, and the center placed the call. At first Ginger responded as she usually did, suspicious that this was a scam, and her daughter's latest attempt to escape the consequences of her drug use. But being curious, Ginger did agree to meet with Arlene and the rehabilitation counselor the next day to discuss the program further. She was going to make sure that the treatment program had the "real story" instead of whatever Arlene had told them.

Due to the long-term presence of the walls we have put up, we may need to solicit outside input to see ourselves accurately and impartially. We can ask people we trust to give us feedback about their first impressions of us. We can ask family members to point out our walls when they go up, and be open to the feedback even if it is uncomfortable. Remember, you cannot change behavior that you cannot see.

When Ginger arrived the next day it was obvious to the intake counselor that this was not going to be an easy interview. Ginger immediately took charge, laying out Arlene's history of drug use and manipulation to

make sure we were all on the "same page." This was obviously painful for Arlene, and it was hard for her not be defensive and at one point looked at the counselor and said, "See?" However the counselor believed that Ginger wouldn't be there if she didn't love her daughter and she didn't want her to get help, and so persisted in the interview. When Ginger had "laid it all out," the counselor turned the interview to Arlene, and supported Arlene to address her mother's concerns with the least amount of defense as possible. Arlene acknowledged all that she had put Ginger through, acknowledging that she had cost her mother loss of sleep and worry, even if it had come out as anger. As Arlene stayed level and did not become combative, Ginger could feel her heart begin to thaw a little, and she saw glimpse of the child she had adored when Arlene was growing up.

Reluctantly, Ginger admitted that she was worried and afraid of being "used" by Arlene, and mostly afraid of getting her hopes up. She acknowledged that she had prepared herself years ago to get a call from a coroner that Arlene had overdosed, and had felt like she was living in suspended animation all this time. In fact, she went so far as to say it might have been better to just get that call and end the anxiety she was living with.

As hard as it was to hear for Arlene, she was able to see and hear her mother as another person, a grieving parent, and Ginger now appeared human to Arlene. She could feel compassion for her Mother and grief for the years they had lost due to Arlene's addiction.

How to establish healthy boundaries

In order to establish healthy boundaries between yourself and others, you need to:

First: Identify the symptoms of your boundaries currently being or having been violated or ignored.

Second: Identify the irrational or unhealthy thinking and beliefs by which you allow your boundaries to be ignored or violated (e.g. It's not important, or I'm just whining).

Third: Identify new, more rational, healthy thinking and beliefs which will encourage you to change your behaviors so that you build healthy boundaries between you and others (e.g. I have a right to respectfully express a concern even if it makes someone else uncomfortable).

Fourth: Identify new behaviors you need to add to your healthy boundary skills in order to sustain healthy boundaries between you and others (e.g. Not returning phone calls when I am tired or in conversation with someone).

Fifth: Implement the healthy boundary building beliefs and behaviors in your life so that your space, privacy and rights are no longer ignored or violated. (e.g. Paying attention to my emotional and physical responses 'using my internal observer' to guide my responses with others).

CHAPTER TEN

MIND-BODY HEALING FOR CODEPENDENCY

Treatment of the mind-body connection of physical health involves several areas of focus. The following areas may prove helpful for you to address with a counselor or sponsor:

(1) Developmental Issues

- Increasing your trust in the attachment to self and others
- Decrease the sense of personal vulnerability, and increase the willingness to recognize, ask for and accept support.
- Treating and resolving early abuse or neglect will ameliorate the lingering negative effects on physical health from unresolved childhood trauma.
- Examination and "reworking" of your working models for relationships is key, and that means you need to be as honest with yourself as possible, even when it is hard.

How do you accomplish this?

- ◊ Meet weekly with a therapist and explore the areas you have noted in this text
- Become an active member of Twelve Step group or other community support group
- ◊ Work with a Twelve Step Sponsor
- Become a member for a formal therapist group led by a professional facilitator

(2) Behavioral Responses

- Strengthen your Internal Observer to increase attunement with yourself and others.

- Notice defense mechanisms that are used to manage anxiety, and increase your ability to internally regulate your emotions through recognizing, acknowledging and expressing them.

- Decrease your reliance on compulsive use of substances or behaviors to artificially soothe, distract or excite internal states.

How do you accomplish this?

◊ Implement some of the ideas outlined in Chapter Ten

◊ Keep journal to become aware of what is happening for you emotionally, behaviorally, intellectually, and spiritually

◊ Experiment with new activities or hobbies to provide stimulation and relaxation

◊ Ask people you trust for feedback when they notice your defensive behaviors

◊ Enroll in a conflict management class

◊ Enroll in a stress management or mindfulness class

(3) Biological Consequences

- Increase your ability to consciously relax and to reverse the habituated stress (fight or flight) response.

- Increase your sensitivity to bodily needs and implement the resulting self-care and self-protection needed to be physically healthy.

- Treat neglected medical symptoms and conditions that you have not "bothered" to address, and create opportunities for your body to experience regular movement in some form.

- Provide your body the nutrition it needs to function well, and create a sleep hygiene program that will support solid, regular sleep.

How do you accomplish this?

◊ Develop meditation and relaxation strategies to "take down" you adrenal system

- ◊ Keep a food an exercise journal to notice how your body is changing and responding
- ◊ Get a yearly physical and follow-up on recommendations
- ◊ Get a dental exam
- ◊ If you have ongoing sleep issues, get a sleep study and get into solution for long-term successful sleep
- ◊ Learn to grocery shop, and make healthy food available to yourself on a regular basis

How Therapy and Cognitive Changes Can Create Neurological Changes:

Recreating Our Past In the Present
http://www.youtube.com/watch?v=HzI5vLBrX8A&feature=related

Let's Make It Personal: Create a Treatment Plan

Everyone will have a different combination of developmental, behavioral, and biological symptoms that require attention. Treatment plans for healing need to be update regularly, so it is a work in progress.

I would encourage you to spend some time creating a plan for yourself, even if you start out with just one thing on each line. Spending the time to parent yourself from a compassionate place is part of the healing process.

Developmental Issues:

_____

_____

_____

_____

_____

_____

Behavioral Issues:

_____

_____

_____

_____

_____

_____

_____

Biological Issues:

_____

_____

_____

_____

_____

_____

_____

Conclusion

I hope this small book has been helpful to you as you work your way through what is, for most of us, a multi-generational difficulty with attachments that are not always obvious. However with our children they are looming – because it feels s though our heart is walking around outside our body. It is unique bond, one that at times defies language. I hope that you will seek out the support of Al-Anon groups like "Parents Letting Go", and invest in your own healing because it is possible to have sanity even if they remain addicted. You were incredibly brave to raise children, knowing there was no guarantee of the outcome. Whatever choices your adult children may make on their journey, YOU are different because you had children. You have wisdom you could not have gained any other way, and there will be way for you to pass it on.

CHAPTER ELEVEN

RESOURCES FOR PARENTS OF ADULT CHILDREN OF ADDICT/ALCOHOLICS

Online Resources:

Hope Networks (Al-Anon On-Line) www.hopenetworks.org/ addiction/alcohol/Al-Anon_Helps_Parents_Alcoholics.html

Survival Kit for Parents of Alcoholics
A group of talks that have helped many Parents learn to live with alcoholism. http://storiesofrecovery.org/Parents.htm

Description:
www.eons.com/groups/group/parents-of-adult-drug-addicts

This group is for Parents and loved ones of Adult Addicts. Our members share a common experience. Our goal is to provide support, understanding, comfort and compassion to those who also deal with the addict in their lives. (20 and over only please).

Families & Friends Of Addicts Support Group
http://www.dailystrength.org/c/Families_and_Friends_Of_Addicts/forum/4905427-my-adult-son-addicted/page-2

Living with adult children
www.cyh.com/HealthTopics/HealthTopicDetails.aspx?p=114&np=99&id=1511#6

Mothers of Addicts United
www.mothersofaddicts.com/Other_Mothers_Tears.htm

Addicted Family Systems:

Another Chance: Hope and Health for the Alcoholic Family Sharon Wegscheider-Cruse

Addict In The Family: Stories of Loss, Hope, and Recovery. Beverly Conyers

It Will Never Happen to Me: Growing Up With Addiction As Youngsters, Adolescents, Adults by Claudia Black

Bradshaw On: The Family: A New Way of Creating Solid Self-Esteem by John Bradshaw

Breaking Free of the Co-Dependency Trap by Janae B. Weinhold Ph.D., Barry K. Weinhold

Letting Go of Adult Children:

Letting Go of Our Adult Children: When What We Do Is Never Enough by Arlene Harder

When Our Grown Kids Disappoint Us: Letting Go of Their Problems, Loving Them Anyway, and Getting on with Our Lives by Jane Adams

Making the Best of It: Building on the Bonds Between Parents and Adult Children by M. Ruth Whybrow

Setting Boundaries(TM) with Your Adult Children: Six Steps to Hope and Healing for Struggling Parents by Allison Bottke

Letting Go (Fifth Edition) by Karen Levin Coburn and Madge Lawrence Treeger

About Setting Boundaries with Your Adult Children:

SANITY (Video) www.youtube.com/watch?v=nhyDxoM03-4

Setting Boundaries with Your Adult Children (Powerpoint)
www.saintjudes.org/adulted/handouts/AdultChildren(1-10-10).pdf

What does "Letting Go" Mean?
From: Letting Go Of Our Children by Arlene Harder

Chapter 8: Letting Go With Love
www.support4change.com/relationships/letgo/8/26.html

Reaching this final stage on the path to healing is like discovering, after a strenuous hike, that the path near the top of the mountain is gentler than we had expected. The tasks we need to accomplish here, while still challenging, are so much easier now that we have moved through the other stages. We are finally prepared to let go with love. An adult-to-adult relationship — and peace of mind — is right around the corner.

As pointed out earlier, letting go involves the process of transferring responsibility for our child's life from *us* to *them*. We move our focus from that of being *parents* to that of being *peers*. In letting go we de-emphasize the parent-child aspect of our relationship, although our family connection will always be part of the equation.

This process of letting go involves learning to treat our children as adults, just as we treat our friends as adults. In fact, an ideal adult-to-adult relationship with our children can be modeled on the ideals of friendship.

While our friends probably share most of our values and lifestyles, many of us have at least a few friends whose views on life are quite different from ours. We may not see these people on a daily basis, but when we are together we enjoy their company and don't try to talk them into being other than who they are, or require them to live out our dreams or fulfill an arbitrary set of expectations. We can have equally satisfying relationships with adult children who are also out of sync with us in some way.

If we've known a friend since childhood, we will, of course, share more memories with that person, but part of what makes friendships work is the attention that is given to the *present* rather than the past or future. Realizing this can encourage us to work toward keeping our interactions with our children more centered in the here and now. And by focusing on what is happening today, we allow both ourselves and our child to evolve into the people we want to be tomorrow, rather than constricting our perceptions by how we viewed one another in the past.

A bit of practice will be needed before these new behaviors become second nature. It will take time, just as it has taken time to work our way through the other stages. Yet our efforts will be rewarded when we accept our child just as he is, in the same way we accept our friends just as they are.

Incidentally, all of the suggestions for letting go with love apply not only to those children in whom we are disappointed in some way but to all our other children as well.

Being a Friend to Our Child

What we expect from our friends we should be able to expect from our adult children — ; and what our friends expect from us, our children should be able to expect from us. It's a two-way street.

If it is impossible, however, for you to have any real connection with your child no matter how hard you try, or if your child has died, your letting go with love will need to involve the process of closure, which is discussed in the next chapter. Nevertheless, understanding the principles that guide friendships can provide the underpinning for that kind of healing as well.

The following are seven expectations we have of our friends. Notice "friends" can refer to adult children and "they" and "them" can refer to either friends or adult children.

We expect our friends to be there when we need them, if possible.

If our daughter needs to borrow our car because hers is in the shop, it's not unreasonable for us to loan her ours - if we can afford to spare it. If we need a bedroom painted and our son knows how to paint, it is not unreasonable to ask whether he would be willing to help us out - provided he can spare the time and wants to help in that particular project. We often have a *quid pro quo* with our friends, helping each other in times of need, and we can work toward that arrangement with our children.

Our reciprocity with friends recognizes their right to decide what *they* will do with their time, money, and energy. And they respect *our* right to make decisions concerning what we will do. With our children, however, a major stumbling block to letting go can be our assumption that we are somehow required to respond to our child's every request if we are going to be loving parents. Likewise, we can assume our children will always be there for us. Then when they don't respond as we would like (in everything from the number of phone calls to the gifts they give), our hurt response can leave them feeling guilty. And when we don't respond as *they* would like, *we* feel guilty. Yet nowhere is it written that parents must loan their child a car just because she asks for it. Nowhere is it written that children must jump whenever their parents need help or feel a bit lonely.

We do not have the right to demand anything from our children, not even love. We can *ask*. We cannot *demand*. When we demand that our child act in a certain way or have a particular value (a demand we may express outwardly or simply feel inside), we attempt to deny them their right to decide how they will spend their time, money, or energy. We deny them their right to think for themselves.

One way you can avoid feeling upset and hurt when your child has not responded to your wishes is to notice what it is that you wanted him to say or do. Then make a statement to yourself of what you would have preferred him to say or do. The operative word is "prefer." Take my case as an example.

I would like Matthew to keep us informed of what he is doing and not wait for us to drive seven hundred miles to see him. If I consider my desire for closer contact as an expectation that he *must* or *should* think of us more often, I will experience a deep sense of disappointment. If he almost never gets in touch with us except when he wants something from us, it can seem almost as though he has disobeyed a law from the center of the universe, or wherever the source of "musts" and "shoulds" is located. If, however, I say that, "I prefer that Matthew give our family more consideration and wish he would stay in touch more often," I do not have nearly as strong of a reaction. The operative word here is "prefer." Unlike "should," "must," and "ought to," which are words of demand, *prefer* implies that the other person has the right - and responsibility - to decide what he will do.

We expect our friends to respect our privacy, just as we respect theirs.

A parent I interviewed told me that she has certain rules for herself about how she will relate to her four grown children. For instance, she said, "We always call before going to our children's houses. To do otherwise would be to treat them as though we had a right, just because we are their parents, to expect them to be there for us." Perhaps you feel perfectly content having friends drop in to visit, whether or not your house is a disaster zone. Your children may share your philosophy. But if you wouldn't want *your* friends (and especially not your own parents or in-laws) to drop in unannounced, don't expect your children to be thrilled when you do it.

The same goes for asking our children how much they are making or how much they have spent on some item we are sure is beyond the range of their budget. Curiosity can kill a cat, and if we aren't careful, it can also screw up perfectly good relationships.

We expect our friends to accept us as we are, including our imperfections, and we accept them as they are. We take pleasure in sharing the victories and defeats that are an inevitable part of every person's life.

A major advantage of letting go is the relief of no longer needing to pretend that we are perfect parents, or perfect people. We no longer have to work so hard to demonstrate that we love our child uncon-ditionally, as many parents assume they must. On second thought, perhaps parents are asked to *love* their children unconditionally, but they certainly aren't required to *like* them unconditionally.

Our children aren't required to like us, either. They don't need to enjoy our music or friends or opinions. We need not be offended if they are bored at our parties, or if we are bored at theirs and find the background music much too loud for our taste. Having a comfort-able relationship doesn't mean we abandon our values and personal tastes or suspend our judgment. We only need to be willing to view each other with compassion, without illusions or expectations.

Once we're willing to accept each other just as we are, we can stop being defensive. Our children can stop being defensive as well. We can learn to be satisfied with a brief visit from our children during which we are genuinely comfortable in each other's presence, rather than insist on doing things together because that is what we believe good parents and their good adult children are *supposed* to do.

Remember that we can be "right" or we can have a relationship of respect and trust. *We can't have both.*

We expcct our friends will respect our desire not to discuss certain topics and we allow our friends to keep some topics off-limits.

If you and your child have diametrically opposing views on certain issues, such as abortion, it is understandable that talking about them is not going to change either of your minds. If either of you insists on bringing up the subject, you will both continue to feel you are getting nowhere. Avoiding such pointless discussions only makes good sense.

If there are topics that cause you pain, it is perfectly okay for those topics to be out of bounds until you are ready to discuss them. In fact, you can do more than *hope* that these topics won't come up;

you can ask your child, directly, not to bring up subjects that have proven divisive in the past.

Similarly, if your child asks you not to discuss some topic, you must honor her request, even though you may be sorely tempted to give her one more "lesson." After all, would you force your friend to talk about something if she didn't want to? Well, maybe you might, rarely, if you had a particularly good friend who was avoiding looking at something that could cause her a great deal of grief if it weren't faced, even though it was a sensitive issue. But my observation of parents and adult children is that parents frequently insist on initiating topics they know their child doesn't want to discuss with them in the hope they can steer him away from trouble (the I'm-only-saying-this-for-your-own-good method of controlling our children).

On the other hand, in choosing to have some subjects "off limits," be careful you don't decide to avoid talking about *any* difficult issue. Some topics need lots of airing for understanding and negotiations to occur, even though they are not comfortable subjects to discuss. But there can come a time when you may realize that more talking isn't going to resolve the issue, especially one that does not require mutual agreement or negotiation but is only a ploy to get the other person to change her mind. Give yourself and your children a break.

We do not expect friends to be the only source of connection, learning, love, and nurturing in our lives.

There are two ways in which we can apply this characteristic of friendships to our relationship with an adult child.

First, unless we work at maintaining lives that are rich and rewarding apart from our role as parents, we will find it difficult to release our children.

Carolyn G. Heilbrun, a professor at Columbia University for more than thirty years, addresses the need for women to use this time of life as an opportunity "to take risks, make noise, be courageous, become unpopular." The same can be said of men. In other words, we need to design our lives so they have meaning and purpose. In an article in the *Los Angeles Times Magazine* in 1992, Heilbrun notes that at a certain age, "there is no longer time for meaningless conversations, for social events where time merely passes, where obligations no longer important are merely fulfilled. One leaves one's space to take part in something that, if ever so slightly, changes the world."

When we no longer count on friends, or children, to provide the basis for all our social needs, we not only experience a richer and fuller life, we have more to share with our friends — ; and with our children.

Second, we must keep reminding ourselves that our child may only be able to learn what he needs to learn *after* we have let him go. There are other sources of learning besides the home.

Consider the case of Jerry, who used drugs during most of high school, dropped out, and showed no inclination to "grow up" while he was living at home. I heard of Jerry's interesting odyssey in maturity when I interviewed his parents, John and Elizabeth. John said that when Jerry was nineteen, he sold the car his parents had given him and went to Hawaii to work and to "find himself." It didn't seem to John that his son was likely to mature when bumming around without parental control, although he and Elizabeth hadn't had much success up to that point in steering him in a different direction. In any case, there was nothing Jerry's parents could do about it.

When he returned two years later, however, they were in for a surprise. John quickly realized that the time away had been well spent. As Jerry walked into the kitchen, where a bowl of fruit was sitting on the table, he asked, "May I have a banana?" John says he knew right then that his son finally saw himself as an adult, not as a child with automatic rights to take from them whatever he wanted. Events since then have reaffirmed the value Jerry received in leaving home when he did.

Find a Metaphor that Works for You

Some parents consider children clay they must mold into a specific shape. When their children are young, that philosophy may sometimes work. However, conflict arises when the parents discover the clay has a mind of its own and resists their attempts at molding. Others see babies as cute toys designed to provide them with pleasure. Again, when their children are quite young, that philosophy may be okay for awhile, but what happens when the toys rebel and resist the role of plaything for narcissists?

The metaphoric way in which we experience our children has a great deal to do with the difficulty or ease with which we can let them go.

If you regard your children as appliances that come with a warranty and must perform as expected, you may want to discard them when they start costing a bit more to support and don't function the way you thought they should. And if you see children as cars you have carefully maintained for years and assume that their performance will reflect on how well you maintain them, you may feel especially responsible if they don't work in top condition when you sell them to someone else eighteen years later.

On the other hand, do you share the view of Erma Bombeck who sees children as kites? Throughout their childhood you keep trying to get them off the ground. You run with them until you're both breathless and still they crash. You patch them up and run again, adding a longer tail. They hit a tree and you climb up to retrieve them. You patch once more, adjusting for their growing size, and caution them about the perils of unseen wind. When they are ready to try their final flight, you let out the string with joy and sadness because you know the kite will snap the line that bound you together. But you also know the kite will fly as it was meant to fly, alone and free.

A slight modification on the kite motif is one that I saw in the home of parents I interviewed for this book. In the kitchen hung a poster of a hot air balloon with the caption, *"There's freedom in loving. To love something completely you must be able to let it go."* At the bottom of the poster she had attached the high school tassels of each of her children. She believed their basic character was set by the time they were eighteen. By then she realized she had to let them go, watch what they would make of the character she had worked to instill in them, and stand back to see where their balloons would land.

It is difficult to let go of the kite or balloon that is our child if we doubt our child's ability to steer a course away from electric wires and other obstacles waiting to snatch the unwary. But unless we keep our child tied down and imprisoned, we don't have any other choice than to let go.

All Your Children Are Equally Important

Several years ago my daughter and I paid a condolence visit to the home of friends whose son had been murdered. After the visit my daughter was very upset with me — ; and for good reason! I had once again talked about Matthew more than I did about our other children. She accused me of spending more time thinking about him than I did about her or her sister and brother. I knew that in the past I had focused much of my energy on him, but I thought I was over that phase. Apparently not. As other parents have noticed, it doesn't matter how satisfied you feel with your other children, when there is one that is having trouble, that one will preoccupy your mind.

After my daughter's comment, I reflected on what happened during our visit. I realized that talking about my pain was an attempt to convey to my friends that I understood their pain in losing a child. But the situations are very different because my child is alive. My only "loss" is the loss of my expectations. I may have reached the fifth stage of healing in a number of ways, but during that visit I certainly slid back into a previous stage. I decided from then on to be more conscious of how much "air time" I would give to the subject of Matthew or to his siblings. He deserves to be mentioned in conversations about our family, but neither more nor less than the others.

All of our children are important. They all deserve our attention.

FOOTNOTES

1. Bowlby, J. (1979). The Making and Breaking of Affectional Bonds. London: Tavistock.

2. Bowlby, J. (1988). A Secure Base. London: Routledge Publishing.

3. Winnicott, D. W. (1971). Playing and Reality. London: Penguin

4. Donovan, W. L., & Leavitt, L. A. (1985). Physiological assessment of mother-infant attachment. Journal of the American Academy of Child Psychiatry, 24, 65-70.

5. Winnicott, D. W. (1971). Playing and Reality. London: Penguin

6. Greenberg, S., & Mitchell, S. (1983). Object Relations in Psychoanalytic Theory. Cambridge, MA: Harvard University Press.

7. Harris, P. L. (1994). The child's understanding of emotion: Developmental change and the family environment. Journal of Child Psychology and Psychiatry, 35, 3-28.

8. Grossmann, K. E., & Grossmann, K. (1991). Attachment quality as an organizer of emotional and behavioral responses in a longitudinal perspective. In C. M. Parkes, J. Stevenson-Hinde, & P. Marris (Eds.), Attachment Across the Life Cycle, 93-114. London: Tavistock/Routledge.

9. Reed, M. D. (1993). Sudden death and bereavement outcomes: The impact of resources on grief symptomatology and detachment. Suicide and Life Threatening Behavior, 23(3), 204-220.

10. Crittenden, P. M. (1992). Quality of attachment in the preschool years. Development and Psychopathology, 4, 209-241.

11. Crittenden, P. M. (1993). Information processing and Ainsworth's patterns of attachment. Paper presented at John Bowlby's Attachment Theory: Historical, Clinical, and Social Significance. C. M. Hinks Institute, Toronto, Canada.

12. Bowlby, J. (1973). Attachment and Loss: Vol. 2. Separation. New York: Basic Books.

13. Zimberoff, D., & Hartman, D. (2001). Four primary existential themes in Heart-Centered Therapies. Journal of Heart-Centered Therapies, 4(2), 3-64.

14. Dayton, Tian, Ph. D (2007). Emotional Sobriety: From Relationship Trauma to Resilience and Balance, HCI: p. 150-151

15. Peck, Scott. (1998) . TouchThe Road Less Traveled and Beyond: Spiritual Growth in an Age of Anxiety. Touchstone Publishers.l

16. Sroufe, L. A., & Fleeson, J. (1986). Attachment and the construction of relationships. In W. Hartup & Z. Rubin (Eds.), Relationships and Development, 51-71. Hillsdale, NJ: Erlbaum.

17. Bretherton, I., & Munholland, K. A. (1999). Internal working models in attachment relationships: A construct revisited. In J. Cassidy & P. R. Shaver (Eds.), Handbook of Attachment: Theory, Research and Clinical Applications, 89-111. (pg.91) New York: Guilford Press.

18. Caspi, A., & Elder, G. H. (1988). Emergent family patterns: The intergenerational construction of problem behavior and relationships. In R. A. Hinde & J. Stevenson-Hinde (Eds.), Relationships Within Families, 218-240. Oxford, England: Clarendon Press.

19. Bretherton, I., & Munholland, K. A. (1999). Internal working models in attachment relationships: A construct revisited.

In J. Cassidy & P. R. Shaver (Eds.), Handbook of Attachment: Theory, Research and Clinical Applications, 89-111. (pg. 91) New York: Guilford Press.

20. Weinhold, Janae and Barry, Ph.D. (2nd Ed., 2008) Breaking Free of the Co-Dependency Trap. New World Library

21. Bee, Helen and Boyd, Denise. (2004). The Developing Child. (10th ed.). Boston: Pearson.

22. Alen, K. E., & Marotz, L. R. (2003). Developmental profiles (4th ed.). Albany, NY: Delmar. Bullock, J. (2002).

23. Ibid

24. Childhood and Society: By Erik H. Erikson. New York: W. W. Norton & Co., Inc., 1950. pp. 397

25. Ibid.

26. Mellody, Pia, Miller, Andre Wells, Miller, Miller, Keith J. (1989) Facing Codependence: What It Is, Where It Comes from, How It Sabotages Our Lives. Harper and Row.

27. Maunder, R. G., & Hunter, J. J. (2001). Attachment and psychosomatic medicine: Developmental contributions to stress and disease. Psychosomatic Medicine, 63(4), 556-567. p. 556.

28. Lachlan A. McWilliams, Ph.D., and S. Jeffrey Bailey, Ph.D. "Associations Between Adult Attachment Ratings and Health Conditions: Evidence From the National Comorbidity Survey Replication," Acadia University; Health Psychology, Vol. 29, No.

29. Stuart, S., & Noyes, R. (1999). Attachment and interpersonal communication in somatization. Psychosomatics, 40, 34-43.

30. Sroufe, L. A., & Waters, E. (1977). Heart rate as a convergent measure in clinical and developmental research. Merrill-Palmer Quarterly, 23, 3-27.

31. Florian, V., & Mikulincer, M. (1995). Effects of adult attachment style on the perception and search for social support. Journal of Psychology, 129, 665-676.

32. Mikulincer, M., & Florian, V. (1995). Appraisal of and coping with a real-life stressful situation: The contribution of attachment styles. Personality and Social Psychology Bulletin, 21, 406-414.

33. Ognibene, T. C., & Collins, N. L. (1998). Adult attachment styles, perceived social support, and coping strategies. Journal of Social and Personal Relationships, 15, 323-345.

34. Simpson, J. A., Rholes, W. S., & Nelligan, J. S. (1992). Support seeking and support giving within couples in an anxiety-provoking situation: The role of attachment styles. Journal of Personality & Social Psychology, 62, 434-446.

35. House, J. S., Landis, K. R., & Umberson, D. (1988). Social relationships and health. Science, 241, 540-545.

36. Kobak, R., & Sceery, A. (1988). Attachment in late adolescence: Working models, affect regulation, and representation of self and others. Child Development, 59, 135-146.

37. Mikulincer, M. (1999). Adult attachment style and affect regulation: Strategic variation in self-appraisals. Journal of Personality and Social Psychology, 75, 420-435.

38. Magai, C. (1999). Affect, imagery and attachment. In J. Cassidy & P. R. Shaver (Eds.), Handbook of Attachment: Theory, Research and Clinical Applications, 787-802. New York: Guilford Press.

39. Raynes, E., Auerbach, C., & Botyanski, N. C. (1989). Level of object representation and psychic structure deficit in obese persons. Psychological Reports, 64, 291-294.

40. Feeney, J. A., & Raphael, B. (1992). Adult attachments and sexuality: Implications for understanding risk behaviours for

HIV infection. Australia and New Zealand Journal of Psychiatry, 26, 399-407.

41. Kotler, T., Buzwell, S., Romeo, Y., & Bowland, J. (1994). Avoidant attachment as a risk factor for health. British Journal of
Medical Psychology, 67, 237-245.

42. Ciechanowski, P., Dwight, M., Katon, W., & Rivera-Ball,
D. (1998). Attachment classification associated with unexplained medical symptoms in patients with chronic hepa-
titis C. Proceedings of the Second International Attachment
and Psychopathology Conference, Toronto, Canada.

43. Felitti, V. J., Anda, R. F., Nordenberg, D., Williamson, D. F.,
Spitz, A. M., Edwards, V., Koss, M. P., & Marks, J. S. (1998).
Relationship of childhood abuse and household dysfunction
to many of the leading causes of death in adults: The Adverse
Childhood Experiences (ACE) Study. American Journal of
Preventive Medicine, 14(4), 245-58.

44. Weinhold, Janae and Barry, Ph.D. (2nd Ed., 2008) Breaking
Free of the Co-Dependency Trap. New World Library

Just For Today in Al-Anon

Just for today: **I will try to** live **through this day only,**
and not tackle my whole problems at once.
I can do something for twelve hours
that would appall **me if I felt that I had to**
keep it up for a lifetime.

Just for today: **I will be** happy. **This assumes**
to be true what Abraham Lincoln said, that
"Most folks are as happy as they make up their
minds to be."

Just for today: **I will try to** strengthen **my mind.**
I will study. I will learn something useful.
I will not be a mental loafer.
I will read something that requires effort.
Thought and concentration.

Just for today: **I will** adjust **myself to what is,**
and not try to adjust everything to my own desires. I will
Take my "luck" as it comes, and fit myself into it

Just for today: **I will** exercise **my** soul
in three ways: I will do somebody a good turn
and not get found out. I will do at least two things I
don't want to do — just for exercise.
I will not show anyone that my feelings are hurt;
they may be hurt, but today I will not show it.

Just for today: **I will be** agreeable. **I will**
look as well as I can, dress becomingly, talk low,
act courteous, criticize not one bit, not find
fault with anything and not try to improve
or regulate anybody else but myself.

Just for today: **I will have** a program.
I may not follow it exactly, but I will have it.
I will save myself from two pests: Hurry and Indecision.

Just for today: **I will have** a quiet **half hour**
all by myself, and relax. During this half hour,
sometime I will try to get a better perspective
of my life.

Just for today: **I will be** unafraid.
Especially I will not be afraid to enjoy what
is beautiful, and to believe that as I give to the world,
so the world will give back to me.

-Kenneth L. Holmes

MARY CROCKER COOK

If you wish to contact Mary please feel free to call, send an email, or a letter.

Mary Crocker Cook
1710 Hamilton Ave. #8
San Jose, CA 95125.

Phone: (408) 448-0333

Email: marycook@connectionscounselingassociates.com

For more information about Mary's counseling services or presentation topics visit:

www.marycrockercook.com